THE
HBCU
EXPERIENCE
THE SOUTHERN UNIVERSITY SYSTEM
EDITION

Visionary Author: Dr. Ashley Little

Lead Author: Janea C. Jamison, MPA

President Letter: President-Chancellor, Dr. Ray Belton

Foreword Author: Bishop Joseph W. Walker, III

Published By: The HBCU Experience Movement, LLC

The HBCU Experience Movement, LLC
thehbcuexperiencemovement@gmail.com

Ordering Information:
Quantity Sales: Special discounts are available on quantity purchases by corporations, associations, and nonprofits. For details, contact the publisher at the address above.

ISBN: 978-1-7349311-8-1

SOUTHERN
UNIVERSITY
AND AGRICULTURAL & MECHANICAL COLLEGE

Smith-Brown Memorial Union – Suite 205
PO Box 13405
Baton Rouge, LA 70813

As I write this, Southern University and A&M College has just celebrated its 141ˢᵗ year of existence. Participating in activities paying homage to our founders and highlighting the global impact of the university causes me to pause again to reflect on how Southern changed my life.

I often think back to my decisions after my service in the U.S. Army. I viewed the GI bill as a passport, so I traveled to Baton Rouge and entered the doors of Southern. I was a non-traditional, first-generation student who required direction. Yet, with the guidance and through a rigorous educational experience at Southern, I have been able to prevail on many levels and will forever be indebted to this great institution.

As one of our spirit songs goes, "I'm so glad I went to Southern U." The sprawling campus and genuine faculty invited me with open arms to discover pathways I never imagined and to begin an academic legacy in my family. I owed Southern and I never forgot that as I continued my education at other institutions, ultimately earning my Ph.D. Private Belton from Shreveport had become Dr. Belton. Sometimes, I still can't believe it. If you would have told me that I would be a career academician after I hung up my combat boots, I would have laughed. I really would have laughed harder if you would have told me I'd be leading the only historically Black university system in the nation. However, Southern opened my mind to it all.

Throughout my career, I have been engaged in university program development and implementation, recruitment, advising and instruction, to higher education administration, resource development and community outreach. I have been afforded opportunities to develop pedagogical methods that enhance teaching and learning and curricula that respond to the economic and workforce needs of the State of Louisiana. Also, I have enjoyed

subr.edu

III

SOUTHERN UNIVERSITY
AND AGRICULTURAL & MECHANICAL COLLEGE

Smith-Brown Memorial Union – Suite 205
PO Box 13405
Baton Rouge, LA 70813

the occasion to serve on state, regional and national committees and have sought to strengthen my professional skills in ways that would enable me to effectively perform the duties of decision-maker, motivator, mediator, spokesperson and manager of resources. But, most importantly, I am privileged to work on behalf of students. I proudly embrace this duty for all our campuses – Southern University and A&M College in Baton Rouge, Southern University at New Orleans, Southern University Shreveport, the Southern University Law Center, and the Southern University Agricultural Research and Extension Center.

Like in the Army, I've had different ranks within the Southern University System. At Southern University Shreveport, I served in positions such as associate professor, department head, vice chancellor for student affairs, and executive vice chancellor. I was ultimately appointed as chancellor. This journey back home in Shreveport allowed me to experience various levels of teamwork and leadership with I proudly carried with me to dually lead the System and the flagship campus in Baton Rouge. These levels of experience also gave me a great appreciation for every single employee that makes an institution truly work for the advancement of our students and communities. I continue to witness great commitment and dedication from the employees at Southern University from the persons who manicure the grounds to those who advance executive decisions. We are all in the same unit with the same mission.

When I was named president-chancellor — the first person to hold the dual role — I was aware of some of the challenges and I quickly realized that there were some opportunities to improve upon the things that would sustain our institutions.

Southern, like all Historically Black Colleges and Universities, are beacons that have and will continue to be manifestations of the American dream of equal educational opportunities for all,

SOUTHERN
UNIVERSITY
AND AGRICULTURAL & MECHANICAL COLLEGE

Smith-Brown Memorial Union – Suite 205
PO Box 13405
Baton Rouge, LA 70813

regardless of religion, ethnic group, or socioeconomic status. The work that occurs on the campuses of the Southern System shapes the Black middle class nationally and globally. Its overarching mission is draped in its origin and guided by its historical traditions. While it is extremely important to embrace our historic traditions, we must also continue to extend our appeal to a variety of other student groups that have aspirations to obtain a college degree.

We are global citizens in a global marketplace that is ever-evolving. We must continuously adapt and evolve to not only maintain relevancy — as we HBCUs find ourselves still justifying at times — but to grow into an even greater educational force. This is why I presented a strategic plan for the System to my colleagues in 2018: "Fulfilling the Promise: A Pathway to Excellence." This is personal to me. I want more students and employees to experience the same opportunities I've been afforded.

"Fulfilling the Promise," brings us back to just that — a promise. We make a promise to potential, current and former students every day: You have a real chance to attain a quality, impactful education. The plan is the outcome of a concerted and comprehensive effort to further develop a broadened roadmap, or "blueprint," that emphasizes a clearly defined vision and outlines achievable goals that reflect our new mission, direction, and core values.

Our collective core values speak greatly to who we are and yes, who I am.

From the plan and my heart:

Academic Excellence and Integrity: Academic excellence will always serve as the hallmark of our endeavors. We commit to conducting ourselves in an honest, ethical, and credible manner with an unwavering commitment to fairness and doing what is in the best interest of our students, faculty, and staff.

Student-Centered: We commit to being relentlessly student-

subr.edu

V

centered. *We want our students, wherever they come from, to experience our university system as the place where they can pursue their dreams and become global leaders.*

Accountability and Effectiveness: We commit to accountability, fiscal responsibility, and transparency, because these are the requirements of sound stewardship. Additionally, we commit to advancing an evidence-based planning and assessment culture that is focused on continuous improvement and centered on the mission.

Innovation and Creativity: We commit to pushing the boundaries of knowledge and possibility as we celebrate fundamental discoveries and practical applications alike. We recognize the linkage between a quality system of higher education and future economic opportunities for our students.

Diversity and Respect: We commit to honor and preserve the individual dignity of everyone across all levels of the university system. We recognize that diversity is the foundation of our university system and we acknowledge that differing viewpoints can help us anticipate and solve problems. We leverage our differences as strengthens in a continuous, fully engaged quest for improvement and innovation.

Collaboration and Teamwork: We commit to professionalism, civility, and cooperation across the university system to ensure success in achieving our stated common goals. We recognize that we are stronger and more effective when we work together as a team.

Advocacy and Open Communication: We commit to promote a culture of openness where individuals are encouraged to offer suggestions for improvement. We encourage courteous, ethical, and proactive two-way communication. We will always actively advocate for our member institutions.

Our top priorities remain, student access and affordability, academic excellence and student success, institutional effective-

Smith-Brown Memorial Union – Suite 205
PO Box 13405
Baton Rouge, LA 70813

ness and accountability, scholarly research, discovery, and entrepreneurship, fundraising and philanthropic support, improving campus life through infrastructural development, and promoting the Southern University brand through outreach and global engagement. Southern University's progress toward these goals will be measured in our successes and accomplishments in every area of our mission statement. "Fulfilling the Promise: A Pathway to Excellence," aligns the strategic plans of each campus within the Southern University System, further reinforcing our "We Are Southern" hallmark.

Many who read this may feel that my life is all about work. I assure you it's not. I have a loving, close-knit family that I share with my wonderful wife, children and grandchildren — who I would like to say are all very understanding of my unpredictable yet rewarding workday. I'd like to think that they realize I wouldn't be the totality of who I am without Southern.

Prior to my career in higher education, I was a practicing professional counselor and on a day-to-day basis I was engaged with people trying to define their dilemmas. So, I learned very early to maintain or create healthy boundaries and to not take things home. Of course, in this career, things do follow me home. I always believe that better days are always on the horizon and there is always an opportunity to change course.

Great things have happened at Southern since its inception and will continue to happen as long as we stay focused on the mission. I am proud to be a part of this dynamic that continues to change communities for the better. I am even more proud that Southern continues to be a part of me. As a verse in our alma mater states, "Oh, Southern, Dear Southern, I owe my all to thee."

subr.edu

VII

President-Chancellor, Dr. Ray Belton

About President-Chancellor, Dr. Ray Belton

Dr. Ray L. Belton serves as the 10th President of the Southern University System, the nation's only historically black university system. Prior to this appointment, he served as chancellor of Southern University at Shreveport, a leadership role that expanded over 14 years. To date, Belton brings more than 30 years of experience in higher education and administration.

During Belton's tenure at Southern University Shreveport, the university enjoyed unprecedented growth resulting in an enrollment increase of more 156 percent. With Belton at the helm, the university acquired more than $34 million to support capital improvements, including academic structures, student centers, and the first-time development of student apartments (one of only two at community colleges in the state) at the institution.

Belton's success as an effective and dedicated higher education leader continues as he currently serves as president of the Southern University System and chancellor of Southern University and A&M College in Baton Rouge. Under Belton's leadership in this dual role, several new programs and strategic initiatives have been implemented System-wide to increase efficiency, boost enrollment, strengthen teaching and learning, enhance technology, improve student success, expand fundraising and philanthropic efforts, and increase alumni engagement.

Most recently, under Belton's leadership of the System, Southern became one of two institutions in the state of Louisiana to be awarded a license to grow medical marijuana. The Southern University Agricultural Research and Extension Center, along with vendor Ilera Holistic Health Care, has produced both THC and CBD medical marijuana products, making Southern the first historically Black college in the nation to do so.

Over the course of the last four years at Southern University Baton Rouge, both retention and graduation rates have evolved, the enrollment of first-time freshman has increased by an average of 15 percent, and resources to support campus enhancements have grown by 220 percent. In addition, the university has achieved several historic milestones, as noted by the remarkable turnaround of the athletic department ascending from a period when only three collegiate teams were eligible for postseason competition to all 15 teams being eligible for the first time in the history of the institution. Further, Southern University Baton Rouge currently enjoys its highest rate of alumni giving since the university's inception in 1880.

Also, under Belton's leadership, the university has experienced unprecedented infrastructural improvements consisting of the establishment of the SU Innovation Center, Jaguar Plaza sports complex, upgrades to athletic facilities. The university was also awarded more than $6 million to support classroom and laboratory improvements, along with curriculum and faculty professional development for the Baton Rouge campus.

Belton has held several national leadership positions, including serving on the Board of Trustees of the Commission on Colleges of the Southern Association of Colleges and Schools, as a Commissioner on Diversity and Inclusion for the American Association of Community Colleges, the Executive Board of the Louisiana Campus Compact, and the National Advisory Board of Community Renewal International. His statewide affiliations include serving in senior leadership roles with the Consortium for Education, Research and Technology (CERT), Biomedical Research Foundation, Alliance for Education, Coordinating & Development Corporation of Northwest Louisiana and as a member of the local Chambers and Committee of 100s.

Early in his career, Belton served on active duty in the United States Army for eight years on assignments stateside and abroad, and was recognized as one of the top non-commissioned officers of his brigade.

Belton has received numerous professional and civic awards. These include: The Leader of the New Century, from the Shreveport Times and the Distinguished Achievement Award, from Kappa Alpha Psi Fraternity, Inc. He is also the recipient of the Thurgood Marshall Community Service Award sponsored by the Black Lawyers Association and is recognized as the "2001 Distinguished

Graduate," University of Texas at Austin. Further, in acknowledging his scholarly work, he was the recipient of: W.K. Kellogg Graduate Fellowship 1996, 1997, 1998; League for Innovation Graduate Scholarship 1996, 1997; C. C. Colvert Scholarship 1997, 1998; John and Suzanne Roueche Scholar 1997, 1998; and Community College Leadership Program Fellowship 1996, 1997.

Belton graduated from Southern University Shreveport and continued his studies at Southern University A&M College, where he graduated first in his class. He earned a Master of Arts in Counseling from the University of Nebraska at Omaha, and a Doctor of Philosophy in Educational Administration from the University of Texas at Austin.

A Message from the Founder
Dr. Ashley Little

Historically Black Colleges & Universities (HBCUs) were established to serve the educational needs of black Americans. During the time of their establishment, and many years afterward, blacks were generally denied admission to traditionally white institutions. Prior to The Civil War, there was no structured higher education system for black students. Public policy, and certain statutory provisions, prohibited the education of blacks in various parts of the nation. Today, HBCUs represent a vital component of American higher education.

The HBCU Experience Movement, LLC is a collection of stories from prominent alumni throughout the world, who share how their HBCU experience molded them into the people they are today. We are also investing financially into HBCUs throughout the country. Our goal is to create a global movement of prominent HBCU alumni throughout the nation to continue to share their stories each year, allowing us to give back to prestigious HBCUs annually.

We are proud to present to you *The HBCU Experience: The Southern University System Edition.* We would like to acknowledge and give a special thanks to our amazing lead author, Janea Jamison, for your dedication and commitment. We appreciate you and thank you for your hard work and dedication on behalf of this project. We would also like to give a special thanks to President-Chancellor Ray L. Belton, Ph.D., foreword authors, expert authors, contributing authors and partners of Southern University System for believing in this movement and investing your time, and monetary donations, to give back to your school. We appreciate all of the Southern University System alumni who shared your HBCU experience in this publication.

Dr. Ashley Little

About Dr. Ashley Little

Dr. Ashley Little is The CEO/Founder of Ashley Little Enterprises, LLC which encompasses her Media, Consulting Work, Writing, Ghost Writing, Book Publishing, Book Coaching, Project Management, Magazine, Public Relations & Marketing, and Empowerment Speaking. In addition, she is an Award-Winning Serial Entrepreneur, TV/Radio Host, TEDx Speaker, International Speaker, Keynote Speaker, Media Maven, Journalist, Writer, Host, Philanthropist, Business Coach, Investor, Advisor for She Wins Society and 13X Award-Winning Best Selling Author. As seen on Black Enterprise, Sheen Magazine (Print and Online), Sheen Talk, Voyage ATL, Fox Soul TV, NBC, Fox, CBS, BlackNews.Com, Shoutout Miami, Shoutout Atlanta, TEDx Speaker, The Book of Sean, HBCU Times, VIP Global Magazine, The Black Report, Vocal, Medium, Soul Wealth, Hustle and Soul, BlackBusiness.com and many more.

She is a proud member of Delta Sigma Theta Sorority Incorporated, and a member of Alpha Phi Omega. She is very involved in her community, organizations and non-profits. Currently, she is the Co-Founder of Sweetheart Scholars Non-profit Organization 501 (C-3) along with three other powerful women. This scholarship is given out annually to African American Females from her hometown of Wadesboro, North Carolina who are attending college to help with their expenses. Dr. Little believes it takes a village to raise a child and to never forget where you come from. Dr. Little is a strong believer in giving back to her community. She believes our young ladies need vision, direction, and strong mentorship. She is the CEO/Founder/Visionary Author of The HBCU Experience Movement, LLC the first Black-owned company to launch books written and published by prominent alumni throughout the world who attended Historically Black Colleges & Universities. As authors, they share a powerful collection of stories on how their unique college experience has molded them into the people they are today. Our company's goal is to change the narrative by sharing Black stories and investing financially back into our HBCUs to increase young alumni giving and enrollment. The Award-Winning Best Selling Authors won the Black Authors Matter TV Award May 2021. Dr. Little is also the Editor and Chief of Creating Your Seat At The Table International Magazine, Advisor for She Wins Society, and Writing and Publishing Coach for the WILDE Winner's Circle.

She is the Founder and Owner of T.A.L.K Radio & TV Network, LLC. Airs in over 167 countries, streamed LIVE on Facebook, YouTube, Twitter and Periscope. Broadcasting and Media Production Company. This live entertainment platform is for new or existing radio shows, television shows, or other electronic media outlets, to air content from a centralized source. All news, information or music shared on this platform are solely the responsibility of the station/radio owner. She is also the Owner and Creator of Creative Broadcasting Radio Station the station of "unlimited possibilities" and Podcast, Radio/TV Host. She is also one of the hosts of the new TV Show Daytime Drama National Syndicated Television Show which will be aired on Comcast Channel 19 and ATT Channel 99 in 19 Middle Tennessee Counties. It will also air on The United Broadcasting Network, The Damascus Roads Broadcasting Network, and Roku. She is CEO/Founder/ Visionary Author of The HBCU Experience Movement LLC and CEO/Founder of Little Publishing LLC.

Dr. Little is a 13X Award-Winning Best Selling Author of "Dear Fear, Volume 2 18 Powerful Lessons Of Living Your Best Life Outside Of Fear", "The Gyrlfriend Code Volume 1", "I Survived", "Girl Get Up, and Win", "Glambitious Guide to Being An Entrepreneur", The Price of Greatness, The Making Of A Successful Business Woman, and "Hello Queen". She is a Co-Host for The Tamie Collins Markee Radio Show, Award-Winning Entrepreneur, Reflection Contributor for the book "NC Girls Living In A Maryland World, Sales/Marketing/ Contributing Writer/Event Correspondent for SwagHer Magazine, Contributing Writer for MizCEO Magazine, Contributing Editor for SheIs Magazine, ContributingWriter/National Sales Executive for Courageous Woman Magazine, Contributing Writer for Upwords International Magazine (India), Contributing Writer/Global Partner for Powerhouse Global International Magazine(London), Host of

"Creating Your Seat At The Table", Host of "Authors On The Rise", Co-Host Glambitious Podcast, Partner/Visionary Author of The Gyrlfriend Code The Sorority Edition along with The Gyrlfriend Collective, LLC and CEO/Visionary Author of The HBCU Experience The North Carolina A&T State University Edition. She has been on many different Podcasts, TV Shows, Magazines, and Radio Shows. Lastly, she has received awards such as "Author Of The Month", The Executive Citation of Anne Arundel County, Maryland Award which was awarded by the County Executive Steuart L. Pittman, Top 28 Influential Business Pioneers for K.I.S.H Magazine Spring 2019 Edition. She has been featured in SwagHer Magazine, Power20Magazine Glambitious, Sheen Magazine, All About Inspire Magazine, Formidable Magazine, BRAG Magazine, Sheen Magazine, Front Cover of MizCEO Magazine November 2019, Front Cover for UpWords Magazine October 2019 Edition, Courageous Woman Magazine, Courageous Woman Special Speakers Edition November 2019, Influence Magazine, Featured/ Interviewed On a National Syndicated Television Show HBCU 101 on Aspire TV, Dynasty of Dreamers K.I.S.H Magazine Spring 2019 Edition, Dynasty of Dreamers K.I.S.H Magazine September 2019 Edition, Front Cover of Courageous Magazine December 2019, Front Cover of Doz International Magazine January 2020, Top 28 Influential Business Pioneers for K.I.S.H Magazine, Power20 Magazine Glambitious January 2020, Power20 Magazine Glambitious February 2020, Featured in Powerhouse Global International London Magazine March 2020 edition, Featured in National Boss Magazine October 2020 Edition, Featured in Sheen Magazine February 2020 as one of "The Top 20 Women To Be On The Lookout For In 2020, BlackNews.com, BlackBusiness.com, Front Cover She Speaks Magazine August 2020, Front Cover National Boss Magazine November 2020, BlackNewsScoop.com, Awarded National Women's Empowerment Ministry "Young, Gifted, & Black Award" February 2020 which honors and celebrate women in business such as Senior Level Executives, Entrepreneurs and CEO's below age 40 for their creativity and business development. Featured in National Women Empowerment Magazine 2020, Featured in

Black Enterprise 2020, Featured on Fox, NBC, CBS 2020, Featured/ Interviewed on National Syndicated Television The Black Report on Fox Soul TV, Front Cover for National Boss Magazine 2020, Speaker at The Black College Expo 2020, Speaker for Creative CEO's summit January 2021, International Speaker for Living Your Dream Life Summit 2021, Speaker for Elite Business Women Powershift Conference 2021, Keynote Speaker/Host/Panelist for The Bella, The Brand & Her Bag Wealth Summit 2021, Speaker for The Unstoppable You Summit January 2021, Speaker for Marketing Mastery Summit for Glambitious 2021, Speaker for Crown Yourself Conference January 2021, Featured in Sheen Print Magazine 2021, Speaker at Door Dash Virtual Black History Month Celebration, Speaker for Day Of Aggie Generations with North Carolina A&T State University, 2021 Woman of Black Excellence Honoree, Guest/ Speaker on podcast The Happy Hour Show, Speaker for the Phoenix Jack & Jill HBCU Author Showcase, Guest/Speaker on The JMosley Show, Contributing Author for "Prayers For The Entrepreneurial Woman Book", Speaker for Creative Con, Recognized as one of Today's Black History Makers, Speaker at From Paper to Profits conference, Press Conference/Press for "Don't Waste Your Petty" Movie, Press Conference/Press for Mahalia Jackson movie, Speaker for HerStory Women's Global Empowerment Summit, Speaker for HerStory Women Who Lead Conference, Speaker for Stepping N2 Sisterhood Sharing Winning Secrets Virtual Summit, Speaker for I AM Glambitious Virtual Conference, Speaker for Black Authors Matter TV show, Speaker for Thought Leaders Global Virtual Summit, Speaker for A Conversation with Floyd Marshall Jr., Black Authors Matter TV Award Winner, Speaker for Sheen Talk, Foreword Author for the anthology "It Cost To Be The Boss", Top 50 Most Influential Women recognized by VIP Global Magazine, Speaker at Black Writers Weekend, Speaker on The GameChangers With Angela Ward Show as well to name a few.

Dr. Little received her undergraduate degree in English from North Carolina A&T State University. Next, she received her Master's Degree in Industrial Organizational Psychology. She has received her Doctorate in Humanitarian and Leadership as well. Dr.

Little is a mover and shaker and she continuously pushes herself to be better than she was yesterday. She gives GOD all the credit for everything that has happened in her life. She has strong faith and determination to be great. She believes her only competition is herself. Her favorite scripture is Philippians 4:13 "I can do all things through Christ who strengthens me".

Table of Contents

Bishop Joseph Warren Walker, III

Foreword
Bishop Joseph Warren Walker, III

I consider it an honor to have this opportunity to share my HBCU story among such an incredible array of excellence. I am humbled by the journey and the lessons I have learned along the way. I pray my story serves as inspiration and enlightenment to those who unrelentingly and unapologetically strive for greatness.

It started in Shreveport, Louisiana. I was born in a God-fearing home the 9th of 10th children. My father owned a House-cleaning service and my mother taught Special Education at a middle school. A strong work ethic and the importance of education were instilled in us all at an early age. I would be tested for Special Education in the 3rd grade because my teacher said I had behavioral problems. I would take the test and it would reveal that I was bored and actually gifted. My parents put drums sticks in my hands and harnessed that energy in a positive direction. That is how my HBCU story began.

It would be music that would motivate and discipline me. Music served as the catalyst that would send me to Southern University. I came to Southern on a band scholarship to march in the band under the late Dr. Isaac Greggs. My experience in that band taught me the value of time and excellence. I could still hear him say, "be in the right place at the right time with the right equipment ready to concentrate." And he would always tell us "if you are on-time you're late." These values would carry over into the classroom and would motivate me to achieve. The community at Southern was so supportive. The intellectual and cultural exposure was priceless and would put me on a path of high achievement that continues to this day.

Today I serve as Pastor of the Mount Zion Church of Nashville, Tennessee. After receiving my Bachelors in English from Southern, I came to Nashville to pursue a Masters of Divinity degree from Vanderbilt and I would subsequently be called this church of 175 members. Mt. Zion currently has over 30,000 members in 3 locations and a global/virtual following that reaches millions each week. I received my Doctorate from Princeton University. I serve as International Presiding Bishop of the Full Gospel Baptist Church Fellowship. I have the honor of serving on two HBCU boards; Meharry Medical College and I Chair the board of Trustees for Tennessee State University. I serve on the board of Citizens Bank, the oldest black bank in the United States. I've authored 13 books and host one of the fastest growing leadership Podcast in the United States called "Next Level Leader".

I am married to Dr. Stephaine Hale Walker, MD, MPH, who is a Neonatologist and Health and Beauty Entrepreneur, and we have 2 beautiful children, Jovanni (9) Joseph (3). My passion is inspiring the next generation. I have been honored to be a lecturer and commencement speaker for several universities. My greatest passion is giving back. My wife and I have given hundreds of thousands of dollars to deserving students who attend HBCU's and we are committed helping students realize their dreams. My mantra remains, "To whom much is given, much is required". I'm grateful for my HBCU experience at Southern University Baton Rouge and will continue to support the mission of all HBCU's as they educate and empower generations to come. I am Southern!

About Bishop Joseph Warren Walker, III

Bishop Joseph Warren Walker, III, is the senior leader of the historic Mt. Zion Baptist Church of Nashville, Tennessee. He was born in Shreveport, Louisiana to Deacon Joseph and Mrs. Rosa Walker.

Bishop Walker received a Bachelor of Arts degree from Southern University in Baton Rouge, Louisiana; a Master of Divinity degree from Vanderbilt University and a Doctor of Ministry degree from Princeton Theological Seminary. He holds three honorary Doctorates from Meharry Medical College, Southern University, Kentucky State University, respectively.

Dr. Walker currently serves on the Board of Directors for Meharry Medical College and Citizens Savings Bank & Trust. In October 2016, he was appointed by former TN Governor Bill Haslam to serve as Chairman of the Board of Trustees for the Tennessee State University, where he has since been unanimously re-elected in 2019. He is also a member of the Omega Psi Phi Fraternity and the Kappa Kappa Psi Band Fraternity.

Bishop Walker currently serves as the International Presiding Bishop in the Full Gospel Baptist Church Fellowship. In July 2013, he was chosen to succeed the founding International Presiding Bishop Paul S. Morton, Sr.

In 1992, at the age of 24, Bishop Walker began his pastorate at Mt. Zion with 175 members. Presently, the ministry has grown to over 30,000 and continues to grow at a phenomenal rate of over 1,000 souls per year. Under his leadership, Mt. Zion has expanded beyond its original location on historic Jefferson Street to eight weekly services in three physical locations and also includes a worldwide virtual church location, Mt. Zion Anywhere, which ministers to millions around the world, as well as a weekly broadcast on that reaches 15 millions viewers worldwide.

A prolific writer, Dr. Walker is a best-selling author of twelve books. Restored at the Root, his latest literary piece, shows you how to deal with life issues not just from a spiritual perspective but a practical landscape. This book goes a step further by discussing the intersection between spiritual authority and clinical spiritual counseling. That way, you can identify the underlying issues at work, which can help save your life, marriage, and family. He and his wife, Dr. Stephaine, co-authored a book together entitled, Becoming A Couple of Destiny.

His inspirational messages make him a sought-after university commencement speaker and orator in diverse spaces. Bishop Walker is a regular guest on the Rickey Smiley Radio Show as well as a host of other nationally syndicated radio shows that reach millions across the United States. He also has been a guest on CNN, Politics Nation with Al Sharpton on MSNBC, The CBS Morning News, CBN, the 700 Club, Sister Circle, The Roland Martin Show and authors a monthly Op-Ed in the Tennessee Tribune, entitled, Reset.

He is married to the former Dr. Stephaine M. Hale, a health & beauty entrepreneur who recently retired as an Assistant Professor of Pediatrics and Neonatology at Vanderbilt University. Both agree that their most joyous accomplishments to date has been the birth of their daughter, Jovanni Willow, who was born in May 2012, and their son, Joseph Warren Walker, IV, born February 2018.

Janea C. Jamison, MPA

O, to Be a Jaguar
Janea C. Jamison, MPA

"O, to be a Jaguar! You know, legend has it that God must be a Jaguar... that's why He made the sky blue and the sun gold."

Like many Black families in south Louisiana, there's a traditional rivalry between two of our largest HBCUs: Grambling University and Southern University. My parents introduced me to the Jaguar Nation at the young age of three years old. What I appreciate the most about Southern University is the tradition. I remember the comfort and excitement of my very first game like it was yesterday. The calmness of the soft wind, the sound of the best band in the land, and the beauty and precision of the fabulous dancing dolls set me ablaze. There was indeed no other feeling that could top the joy of attending my first SU homecoming. It set the tone of what it means to embody Black excellence and greatness. I continued to look forward to Southern University's Homecoming and Bayou Classic games throughout my adolescent years. My mom is a proud 1976 graduate of Southern University, and she always shared stories of her tenure on "the yard." She often described her experience on campus as her very own utopia.

I yearned to have that same feeling one day. Outside of those football games, my immediate family and church, I had minimal exposure to Black culture. For fifteen years (Pre-school - 12th grade), I attended private predominately white Catholic schools. I am very appreciative of the sacrifices of my parents and the privilege of attending Catholic school. My Catholic upbringing is also a part of who I am. It laid the foundation of my faith. But I always felt something was missing. I missed the experience of having representation in the school system and seeing adults who looked like me. In many situations, I was one of few Black students. The majority of my friends were White. Those I saw in positions of authority or power were also White. My entire view and perception of the world were primarily shaped by Europeanized culture. So, the choice to attend a Historically Black College and University was relatively easy.

Off to the Yard

In May of 2008, I graduated from Ascension Catholic High School with a 3.8 GPA. I also ranked top 7 in my class. I seriously thought the world was mine with a window of opportunities! I applied to a few schools, but the only college I looked forward to attending was Southern University. Oh, how excited I was once I received my acceptance letter! My first SU experience as an "adult" was "Jaguar Preview." Jaguar Preview was freshman orientation the summer before the fall semester. I was so excited about that weekend. I finally had the chance to experience Southern without my parents' supervision. I got an idea of what campus life would be like on my own. Although I am extremely outgoing, for some reason, I became shy and timid at the fact that I would have to make all new friends. I had two best friends in high school, but they decided to go to Xavier University. Here I was, a young Catholic schoolgirl from the deep, rural south, ready to take on Southern University. I was fortunate enough to make solid friendships from Jaguar Preview that would last a lifetime. The entire summer, we remained in contact and planned to room together on campus in the fall.

Anticipation grew deep leading up to August of 2008, the start of my first semester. Before our official move-in day on campus, my friends and I met at the McDonald's at the corner of Scenic Highway and Harding Boulevard right outside campus. We all stood there, bright-eyed and bushy-tailed with our parents, ready to take on Southern University and move into S.V. Totty Hall. In my eyes, the campus was *huge*! It was filled with promising young students who looked like me but came from various cultures and backgrounds. I was so eager to have my "A Different World" experience.

Campus Life and Extracurriculars

As I stood in line, waiting for my dorm room number, I was approached by a familiar face. I was so excited to see someone I had known before freshman orientation. She was currently a senior. In fact, she was Miss Senior. Miss Senior and I had a similar background, attending the same private high school and being raised in a small, rural community. I was thrilled to have a familiar face to confide in. It was good to have someone provide me with sound advice. Once I settled in and adjusted to campus life and friends, the current Miss Senior encouraged me to run for Miss Freshman.

She said, "In high school, I became accustomed to looking to my right, and you were by my side. I would feel awkward if I looked down to my right and didn't see you as Miss

Freshman." Those words resonated with me and motivated me to embark on a new journey: Miss Freshman 2008-2009. I didn't want to let down Miss Senior, but I was uncertain If I would be a good face for my class. I wasn't sure if people would like me. I also wasn't sure of the amount of time and effort it would take to run my first SGA campaign. But I didn't allow those uncertainties to stop me.

I had about $500 of unused scholarship funds. The encouragement from Miss Senior and my mother allowed me to lead my first successful SGA campaign. I used my platform as Miss Freshman to vocalize students' concerns to the board, host beautification projects around campus, and assist Miss Southern University with her St. Jude Children's Hospital initiatives. Being Miss Freshman taught me to step outside of the box. It taught me to never be afraid to try new things simply because I didn't know the outcome. It also allowed me to broaden my network within the Southern University system as I met students at SUNO and SUSLA. That spring semester, I even had my first campus job. I worked at the Southern University Ag Center. In my freshman year, I also learned the importance of sharing your experiences at an early age. I signed on as an SU Student Ambassador, gave tours to high school students, and expressed my joy in being a Southern University student. As a political science major, I even registered students to vote and organized students to the state capitol during the Bobby Jindal era to protest against the budget cuts.

Being active on campus and utilizing my voice prepared me for my career. I saw the importance and value in speaking up and speaking out. There was so much fulfillment in working for causes much greater than myself.

My sophomore year, I was a fall 2009 initiate of the Beta Psi Chapter of Alpha Kappa Alpha Sorority, Inc. I was introduced to this illustrious sisterhood as a child by attending conventions and Boules with my great aunts. As an Alpha Kappa Alpha woman, I broadened my leadership capabilities and grew a deep love for community engagement and helping others. Being a member of various organizations such as AKA, SGA, SU Student Ambassadors, and others also opened my eyes to the different world outside of campus. Although campus life was great, I noticed the lack of infrastructure and poor leadership within the state of Louisiana. This propelled me even further to "do good and seek justice." I wanted to make a difference and help shape the policies that directly impact people who look like me. I finished undergrad in May of 2012. I graduated Cum Laude with a 3.7 accumulative GPA, which was the second highest in my

department. But I knew this wasn't the end of my educational journey. After a one-year break, I enrolled in the SUMPA (Southern University Master of Public Administration) program. It was through this program that I learned the importance of relationships and networking in the real world. My undergrad and graduate school professors are still like family. My professors encouraged me along the way and poured real-life experiences and knowledge into me. In fact, my former grad advisor connected me to my first job in grad school. Both my undergrad and graduate school HBCU experiences propelled me into my career.

Career and Life

As a 2012 and 2015 graduate of Southern University and A & M College, my HBCU experience allowed me to find my voice and passion for the community. My HBCU experience gave me the tools and resources to continuously change Louisiana's trajectory. It gave me the tools to build pathways for communities of color within the Deep South. I am currently the Director of Programs for the 501(c)3 civic engagement table for the state of Louisiana. My ability to advocate for the freedom and liberation of Black folx, lead statewide campaigns, and create pathways to democracy would not have been made possible if it were not for Southern University. Through Southern, I made lifelong friends who are more like family.

I served in leadership roles, managed campaigns, and served the community. Southern University proved that it is vital to invest in Black leadership and create opportunities for students to reach new heights.

To this day, I still have a close relationship with faculty and students. I am a member of the Southern University Alumni Federation and partner on the SU VOTES initiative. I am forever grateful for Southern University. My lifelong goal is to continue to raise awareness of the importance of attending HBCUs and giving back to our esteemed institutions. I hope that my story will motivate anyone who is shy or intimidated to step out of their comfort zone because the world of opportunities is endless. I will always attribute my success to Southern University and my HBCU experience.

Lead Author Janea C. Jamison, MPA

About Janea C. Jamison, MPA

Entrepreneur, Policy Advocate, Community voice.

Janea is a Louisiana native and hosts a weekly podcast called *Her Story, L.L.C. She* creates opportunities for critical dialogue and action for Black Women who have defied obstacles and turned them into success. Her passion for women empowerment and positive body image is also reflected through her activewear brand, Kloset Fitness, L.L.C., which centers on various designs for women of all sizes.

Janea Jamison is a longtime advocate for race and gender justice. Her justice lens focuses on centering BIPOC women and girls in policy, organizing, and advocacy to develop a roadmap for equity.

Currently, Janea leads all programming strategies for the Power Coalition. Her work includes the statewide growth of the Power Coalition and the implementation of core programming, including She Leads-- a leadership program for female leaders of color; Black Men and Boys Statewide work; voting rights work; and policy/advocacy work. Under Janea's leadership, the Power Coalition lead a successful 2019 statewide Census campaign that utilized a digital informed approach to reach thousands of "Hard to Count" Louisianians across the state during a pandemic.

She also leads a comprehensive Election Protection Program in partnership with NAACP Legal Defense and Educational Fund and The Lawyers' Committee for Civil Rights Under Law.

Prior to her position with the Power Coalition, Janea worked with the East Baton Rouge Metro Council as the Legislative Assistant to Councilwoman Erika L. Green (D-5) and Court System Supervisor in Assumption Parish under the leadership of Mayor Ron Animashaun. Her program areas included constituent relations and youth development. She is a proud member of Alpha Kappa Alpha Sorority, Inc. She received her undergraduate degree in Political Science and Master's in Public Administration from Southern University and A&M College in Baton Rouge, Louisiana. In her spare time, she volunteers for local nonprofits such as Imagination

Leads, Butterfly Society, St. Vincent De Paul, Big Buddy Program, and DreamWorks Louisiana. She is a 2021 Southern University Alumni Federation 40 under Forty Cohort Trois, a 2020 Institute of Politics: Loyola University New Orleans Cohort, and a 2019 BOLD (Black Organizing for Leadership & Dignity) Fellow.

Through a commitment to service to a cause greater than self, she hopes to inspire millennials to take an active stand in their communities.

Dr. Derrick V. Warren

LESSONS FROM MY SOUTHERN UNIVERSITY HBCU EXPERIENCE

By Dr. Derrick V. Warren, Interim Associate Dean and MBA – Southern University – Baton Rouge College of Business; Director of SU System Alumni Affairs and Executive Director of the SU Alumni Federation – SUBR '82 Computer Science

As the son of HBCU graduates (my parents, Calvin and Idell Warren, are graduates of Grambling State University), I was continuously exposed to the power, pageantry, prestige and potential of Historically Black Colleges and Universities (HBCUs). My dad took me to football games; my mom ensured I participated in her sorority events; my aunts and uncles also took every opportunity to impart knowledge and understanding of the importance of education. Since graduating from my beloved Southern University (the only historically black college and university system in the world) over 38 years ago, I realize now more than ever how my HBCU experience not only prepared me for corporate America, but for a global life experience that took from a small town in north Louisiana to some of the largest cities in the world! I tell students that they can go anywhere in the world from Southern University. From Southern University, I traveled to the White House for lunch with the President and to witness the initial signing of the White House Initiative on HBCUs. From Scott's Bluff, I joined and eventually became a corporate Vice President one of the world's foremost technology companies, International Business Machines (IBM). From 'across the hump', I lived abroad and managed Global teams in Tokyo, Shanghai, Seoul, Singapore, Mumbai, Singapore, Shenzhen, Sydney, Melbourne, Hong Kong, Macao, London, Paris, Johannesburg, Cape Town, Beijing, Bangalore, Manilla and other places domestically and abroad. I don't consider myself a 'born leader', but one who received practical 'hands on' training at the foot of Southern giants. While in school I served as: Junior Class and Student Government Association (SGA) President; member of the world renowned SU Human Jukebox; Kappa Kappa Psi Band Honorary Fraternity; Alpha Phi Alpha Fraternity, Inc. Kappa Phi

Kappa Education Honorary and a 3rd Degree Mason of the SU John G. Lewis Lodge. I remain grateful to everyone who played a role in my Southern University experience and those who continue to support my journey today. These God given experiences provided a number of remarkable life lessons. In my current role as Interim Associate Dean and MBA Director/Director of Alumni Affairs, I wanted to focus my story on several of those lessons. Lessons that I would like to share with students and others as they travel through college and life as a whole. It's a call to action that I call "Warren's Wisdom". Warren's Wisdom wants you to:

1. **Be accountable.** You are now in college. You are expected to wake up on your own, clean up behind yourself, be present in class and be responsible for your respective obligations. Own your stuff and no excuses! Do this and your college days will prosper.

2. **Have Fun, but you keep a focus on academics.** You're here to earn a degree. Participate in the full college experience, but do not lose focus on graduation. Make that a priority. It's also very important to participate in organizations that complement your degree and participating in activities that advance your goals.

3. **Practice Self Love, Self-Care, Self-Growth and Self Confidence.** Self-care is very important. Ensure that 'you' are a priority and that you are continuously keeping an eye on your mental and physical health. This includes meditation, exercise and proactively taking steps that keep your mind and body in optimal condition. Also, get regular check-ups, rest and focus on a balanced diet to solidify a healthy lifestyle. Too many students get on campus and in their quest to be liked, end up harming themselves and becoming ill. You are no good to the world if you are not healthy and being your best self.

4. **Don't Give Anyone Permission to Make You Feel Inferior.** Unfortunately, you will meet some people in college and life who will try to tear you down. Rebuke, repel and remove

anyone from your circle who is not constructive in their words and actions toward you.

5. **Find Your "Genius".** I define "Genius" as the intersection of what you love and what you are good at. Some people call it "Purpose". Whatever you call it, find it and be true to it. If you try to be anything other than you, the journey will be very challenging. Figure out what you're passionate about; what you are good at and most importantly what you love and I am sure it will lead you to success.

6. **Be a Problem Solver.** Don't simply point out problems without recommending solutions. Better yet, actively work to solve the problem and ensure it is communicated when the problem is raised. That is what the world and SU need.... more problem solvers and less problem causers.

7. **Fail Forward.** You will make mistakes. Use them as learning lessons to propel you forward.

8. **Be Disciplined and Persistent.** In college and life, you will face pain. The pain of discipline or the pain of regret. As a great author once said, "Choose wisely."

9. **Learn How to Fight.** This lesson isn't about 'laying hands' on someone. It's about the reality that conflict is inevitable. You can't avoid it. Embrace it and learn how to settle, negotiate and talk through disagreements without physical violence. You can disagree without being disagreeable and violent. Ask yourself the question of "Is it worth being put out of school or going to jail?"

10. **Find a Mentor, be a mentor.** In fact, find several mentors. You can't have too many. They serve different purposes; help at different times and have different skills and talents. Everyone needs a guide to help them navigate life (personally and professionally). Do this as soon as possible.

11. **Focus on Relationships and Results.** Don't just network, build relationships with people and companies. Build on those relationships through integrity (saying what you will do

and doing what you say) as well as executing with valuable results. Live. Love. Learn. Laugh. Life sometimes gets this wrong. We have learned to love things and use people. Reverse that. Love people and use things.

12. **Be Very Careful What You Post on Social Media, It Could Impact Your Life and Career.** Stay positive on social media and never post anything that you would not want on the front page of the Wall Street Journal or New York Times. I know of personal examples where people have lost jobs because of things posted on social media.

13. **You Are the Message.** You are the message. You are a brand. What you do and say is a reflection of you and your brand. DO NOT HARM THE BRAND. Always remember, EXCELLENCE Defines Us. PRIDE Sustains Us. TRADITION Guides Us.

14. **Be better today than Yesterday.** This is the essence of growth. Strive to make today, a better day than yesterday and tomorrow, better than today. In fact, help everyone around you do the same. It's a roadmap to a better world.

15. **Be GRATEFUL and PAY IT FORWARD.** You have been the recipient of many gifts. You have also received grace and mercy (grace being unmerited favor and undeserved blessings and mercy being forgiveness for bad things that you have done). Show gratitude to those who have shown you kindness and forgiveness. Pay it forward by showing kindness and forgiveness to others as you go through life. This is one of the best ways to thank those who gifted you.

**EXCELLENCE defines us. PRIDE sustains us.
TRADITION guides us.**

WE ARE SOUTHERN!

Expert Author Dr. Derrick V. Warren

About Dr. Derrick V. Warren

Growing up in a small North Louisiana town taught Derrick the importance of relationships, results and resilience. From a young age, his parents, Calvin and Idell Warren (both HBCU graduates and educators), instilled in him the reality that a quality education is extremely important in life. "Education is a great equalizer in a world that is not always fair", states Dr. Warren. Determined to help bridge the digital divide for under represented communities, this self-described "Global Life Learner" drives positive transformation for Southern University as the Interim Associate Dean and MBA Director for the SU Baton Rouge College of Business. In addition, Dr. Warren is the Director of Alumni Affairs and an Adjunct Professor with specializations in Artificial Intelligence, Blockchain, Cloud Computing, Cyber Security, Data Science, Design Thinking, Internet of Things, Management and Marketing. Prior to his roles at Southern, Dr. Warren spent over 32 years with IBM and was responsible for the overall client satisfaction, financials, and delivery execution of large accounts ranging in size from several hundred million to over a billion dollars in total contract value. He considers himself a global citizen having lived and worked abroad in Asia, Europe the Middle East and Africa. He has also published articles in industry magazines and is an accomplished speaker at business symposiums, conferences, and universities around the world. Dr. Warren, a Computer Scientist by degree, also served as a member of the IBM Technical Leadership Team, IBM Global Services Diversity Council and was featured in the company's "On Demand" Thinker Ad Campaign. This campaign appeared globally in business publications that included Time Magazine, The Wall Street Journal, Forbes, Business Week, The Economist, Money Magazine, Barron's, CIO, CFO as well as other international publications. The recipient of numerous professional and community awards, Dr. Warren was named the National Alumni Director of the Year by the National Black College Hall of Fame in 2018, Jaguar Foundation Man of the Year and honored to deliver Southern's fall 2011 Commencement Address. Dr. Derrick Warren has a Bachelor of Science degree in

Computer Science (cum laude) from Southern University - Baton Rouge, a Master of Business Administration from the University of South Florida in Tampa and a Doctor of Business Administration from the Georgia State University (GSU) Robinson College of Business in Atlanta, Georgia. He and his wife (college sweetheart), Anita, currently reside in Baton Rouge, La. They are the proud parents of two sons, Derrick II and Dillon; daughter, Dhalyn; and granddaughter Emersyn.

Councilwoman Chauna Banks

Southern University: My Family Tradition
Councilwoman Chauna Banks
East Baton Rouge Parish/City of Baton Rouge Metropolitan Council

I can't begin to share my HBCU experience without beginning with my parents, Charlie Banks, Sr. and Estella Square Banks. My father is the oldest of three, and my mother is the oldest of twelve. These are the first college graduates in all of our immediate and extended families. There is where the legacy of Southern University college experiences started in my family.

My maternal and paternal grandparents reared their families in the community of Scotlandville. Scotlandville was a rural village that was once the entry point for the slave trade and home to a cotton plantation. It became the largest majority African American town in Louisiana, located in the northern part of East Baton Rouge Parish.

Scotlandville's history is interconnected to Southern University and A&M College System, the only HBCU system in the United States. Southern University relocated from New Orleans to the bluff of the Mississippi River on the western edge of Scotlandville in 1914.

The bluff is believed to be named after a previous owner, Dr. William Bernard Scott, who bought the property in 1839 from Lelia Skipworth, the daughter of a former governor of the 1810 West Florida Republic. Local legend marks Scott's Bluff as the location of the famous *baton rouge,* or "red stick," from which the city of Baton Rouge got its name.

My mother graduated in the first high school class of Scotlandville High School in 1956. Likewise, my father graduated in the same year from Southern University Laboratory School. Neither of my grandparents knew anything about college. But one of my mother's classmates, Ruby Jean Sims, attended Camphor Memorial Methodist Church in Scotlandville, where a lot of its members were secondary educators and Southern University college professors. Ruby Jean helped my mother register for college at Southern University and choose her major. She recruited her to pledge Zeta

Phi Beta Sorority.

Southern University Laboratory School was a college preparatory institution where students were assigned to gain a semester of practicum experience for a teaching career. But it was my mother's pursuit of a college education that led my father to also enroll at Southern University. Both my parents had long careers as teachers and school administrators before retiring.

There is something to be said about the motto, "When you lead by example, you make it easy for others to follow you." That is exactly what happened with my parents' siblings. Ten of my mother's eleven siblings graduated from Southern University, and one of my father's two sisters is also a graduate. All of my five paternal first cousins are graduates of Southern, and the majority of my maternal college degreed first cousins graduated from there, as well. Now, I am experiencing a third generation of cousins who are a part of the Southern University "Jaguar Nation".

Based on my parents, aunts, uncles and cousins, I didn't realize that everyone did not go to college after high school graduation. Therefore, when I graduated from Southern University Laboratory School in May of 1979, it was natural for me to continue my education at Southern University, as it was passing from one grade to the other.

I was not even aware of other options, such as attending college across town at our state's flagship school, Louisiana State University. I wasn't aware of the option of joining the military, attending trade school, or even getting a full-time job. There was never even a conversation in my home that raised a question about me going to college or enrolling in Southern University.

There was just one problem: I was clueless. I hadn't figured out what I was going to major in. The natural inclination was for me to follow in my parents' footsteps and become a teacher. However, my mother told me she didn't want me to become a teacher because it didn't pay well. In her opinion, as a teacher, "You have to go through too much." It was not that I had settled on a career in teaching. It was just that I didn't have a vast knowledge of different career choices.

Whereas the generation before me was mostly educators, my generation had advanced to pursue such careers as engineering, computer science, accounting, business, marketing and the sciences. All of these options placed me in a predicament. Math and science were my weakness. My strengths were in the areas of liberal arts, which was perfect for a teaching career. However, that was no longer a viable option because of what my mother advised.

I chose to major in computer science, what I rationalized as the lesser of all the evils. To my surprise, I still had to take many of the classes in the other disciplines as part of the computer science curriculum.

Each semester, I took the minimum twelve hours during the fall and the minimum nine hours during the summer. I went to school year-round so I could pass all my classes, drop classes as needed, spend time in The Student Union, and work a part-time job off campus. I graduated on time, in four years, with a bachelor's degree in computer science from Southern University in December of 1983.

The number of computer system jobs increased from 600,000 in 1978 to 6 million in the four years I was in college. However, these jobs were not in Louisiana or any other state in close proximity. Either way, I didn't want to leave home. I really didn't have the confidence to pursue one of these high-tech jobs anyway. For the next seven years, I was gainfully employed, but nothing that would lead to a satisfying career.

At this point in my life, I had gone through a divorce and I had a child. I was working both full-time and part-time jobs. One of my cousins had similar life-altering experiences in her personal life. Upon graduating college, she was told about a graduate program at Southern University in Mental Health Counseling. Afterward, I was constantly thinking about the program. But I could not figure out how I could afford graduate school. I already had major financial responsibilities. I could not quit my part-time evening job to attend the classes offered in the evenings.

Then a miracle happened. I got laid off my full-time job. During the orientation to receive unemployment benefits, I learned of a program called the Job Training Partnership Act (JTPA). The JTPA program was offered by the City of Baton Rouge to increase the employability of economically disadvantaged adults and youths through the development of good work habits and basic work skills. After qualifying for the program, I was told that I would have up to two years to complete education and/or training for job placement.

I immediately met with the Education, Counseling and Leadership Chairperson, Dr. Harry Albert, who confirmed I could complete the graduate program in two years. Then, I met with the Dean of the Southern University Graduate School, Dr. Wilbur Clarke, who offered me a graduate assistant position. I was assigned to the Center for Social Services, where I worked about twenty hours a week under the direction of Dr. Alma Thornton. After almost ten years, I finally discovered my calling. In December of 1993, I earned a master's degree in mental health counseling.

After working ten years for a state agency in child welfare, I received an ancillary certificate in school counseling. My career with East Baton Rouge Parish School System has allowed me to use my life experiences to have a more realistic view on helping students transition from high school to post-secondary education and training. Once my mom saw me thrive, she said to me, "I apologize. I never should have told you not to be a teacher. You should have always had a career in a school system. You probably would have been a principal." From that day forth, my mother always told parents to encourage their children to be whatever they want to be.

I thank God that Southern University was there for my parents, me and my siblings, and my son. We are all Southern University graduates. I currently have a niece at Southern University, and my nephew will be enrolling in the fall. To say that Southern University is intricately embodied in the legacy of my family is an understatement.

In spite of my not-so seamless path, I overcame all my challenges and my wildest dreams manifested because I was in an HBCU environment where graduates thrive in pursuit of purpose and financial well-being.

O' Southern, Dear Southern! You prepared me for life!

About Councilwoman Chauna Banks

East Baton Rouge Metropolitan Councilwoman
Born: December 2, 1961
Birthplace: Baton Rouge, Louisiana

Elected to her third term, Councilwoman Chauna Banks continues to serve as Metropolitan Council member representing Council District 2.

The oldest of 4 children born to Charlie Banks, Sr. and Estella Square Banks. Banks began working at a locally owned grocery store as a cashier when she was 15 years old. She later worked as a store cashier at Woolworth.

A native of Baton Rouge, Chauna graduated from Southern University Laboratory High School (1979) and received her Bachelor of Science degree at Southern University in Computer Science (1983), further graduating from Southern University Graduate School with a Master's degree in Education, Leadership, and Counseling from Southern University School (1992).

In 1985, she married and had one child, but later divorced. As a single parent she reared her son and worked several full-time and part-time jobs in the private sector. After completing graduate school, re-marrying, and a career change, Banks worked for state government before her employment with the East Baton Rouge School System. She has been assigned several positions to include Mental Health Counselor; Graduation Coach; Grants Project Manager; Interim Dean of Students; and Professional School Counselor.

Once again divorced, at age 52, 2013 Banks elected to the East Baton Rouge Parish Metropolitan Council in 2013. She was the first woman to be elected to the seat.

While rooted in a consistent tradition of empowering the underserved, Chauna has crafted a vision for Metro District 2 that focuses on equitable funding for blight elimination, infrastructure, and new housing construction. Creating economic opportunities for her constituent base, whose demographics are continually expanding, is a priority. She has likewise enhanced her district by increasing commercial development, experiencing a reduction in crime, and continuously advocating for healthcare access opportunities.

In 2014, Councilwoman Banks created the Jewel J. Newman Community Center (JJNCC) Advisory Board, whose dedicated support of community center staff has led to enhanced services and established the center as «A Place for All.» Under her leadership, JJNCC has received increased City-Parish funding for building and grounds upgrades.

Chauna has led efforts to increase revenues and a JJNCC Capital Campaign. Proceeds are dedicated to increasing the quality of life for her constituents with such events as a Masquerade Ball, Back-to-School Rally, Senior Appreciation Luncheon, and much more.

Her dedication and hands-on approach with residents, business leaders, public and private institutions, community groups, and other elected officials has been fundamental in changing the "status quo."

The #NBRNow Blue Ribbon Commission, appointed by Councilwoman Banks in 2016, consists of nine members, whose ultimate mission is to enrich north Baton Rouge's communities and economy through public-private partnerships and grass-roots efforts. Two major initiatives being pursued: bringing Champion Medical Center emergency services to Howell Place and keeping the BREC Zoo in its current location with the necessary sustainable resources to promote it as a recreation, education, and conservation destination.

Councilwoman Banks has made a life-long commitment to move her community forward, and will always work to foster an end to joblessness, neighborhood blight, and poor public education through using the tools of public policy, legislation, and public involvement. Her overall vision is to improve her constituents' quality of life — regardless of race, class, gender, or socioeconomic status. She continues to believe that there is a solution to every problem and that when we work together, everybody wins.

Banks is the mother of one adult son and daughter-in-law and has two grandchildren.

Lucina Jamison

A Small-Town Girl with Bigger Dreams
Lucina Jamison

Three things have helped me along this journey called life: God, family and the determination to never give up. My name is Lucina Marie Heim Jamison. Many refer to me simply as "Lou." Growing up in the deep rural south in the Jim Crow era, I came from humble beginnings. I was born on December 28, 1951, at St. Elizabeth Hospital in Paincourtville, Louisiana. Our family home is in Bertrandville. If you haven't figured it out yet, every town is about a mile apart in the country and ends with "ville."

My parents were born and raised in Assumption Parish. My father, Martin Joseph Heim, was of German and Jamaican descent. His father, Jacob Heim, was a white German immigrant who traveled to North Carolina and met a free woman of color by the name of Sarah Postan. Jacob and Sarah somehow traveled to Napoleonville, where my family is still located along Bayou Lafourche today. My mother, Ora Skidmore Heim, was the strongest, most resilient, and intelligent woman I've ever known. I get that boldness, determination and charisma from my dear mother. Now, her family, the Skidmores, owned a decent amount of property in Bertrandville. Growing up, if I wasn't taught one thing, it was to work hard. I was also taught that a man's value was determined by the amount of land he owned and the property he had to pass down to his family. My grandparents, Jules and Jannette Skidmore, did just that. They owned and worked the land.

Times were different back then. Although my mother only had an eleventh-grade education, she is still one of the most intelligent people I've ever known. She was born in 1912, and during those times, intelligence wasn't necessarily determined by your level of education. It was determined by your ability to adapt and seek knowledge on your own.

I was the youngest of five children. Ora, my mother, was a homemaker, and my father, Martin, was a laborer. He worked tirelessly in the sugar refinery. Although my father was of a "mixed" race, that meant absolutely nothing in the South. His parents had to face their barriers being an interracial couple during that time when it was mostly illegal in southern states.

Nonetheless, at a young age, I was more than familiar with the lack of diversity and inclusion, racism, segregation, white supremacy, male patriarchy and classism that permeated throughout the country. It was the root of survival during this period. Although some aspects of the world were filled with hate, my siblings and I were always taught to keep God first and push forward to survive. Unfortunately, at only three years old, I had to do just that. I was forced to move forward when trauma entered my life. On April 5, 1955, my father passed away from a heart attack at the age of forty-six. He left behind my mother and five young children. The oldest, my brother Gerald, became the man of the house at just sixteen years old. They say when tragedy strikes, it never leaves your memory.

I remember my father's funeral like yesterday, from the rain that fell and the lilac dress I wore, to being carried on my brother's hip to the burial. I also felt my father's absence. I would wait on the front porch steps with my sister Lavern, waiting for my father to come home with his red lunch pail. Unfortunately, he would never come home again. Some may say that's a sad story, but tragedy shaped me. It taught me to keep going. It taught me never to give up, and it taught me triumph over adversity. This was also when I saw my mother's willfulness kick in. It was a willfulness to not only survive, but to provide for her children. After my father's passing, once a homemaker, she was hired as "the help" to a "prestigious" lawyer and politician in Assumption Parish. She was only paid $25 a week, but she made ends meet. She also sent all five of us to Catholic school, St. Benedict the Moor School.

My mother sacrificed a lot to raise us. She worked so hard, sometimes seven days a week and even holidays. But my siblings and I never went without anything. We were well-fed, we dressed nice, and we attended mass almost daily. We never even knew we were poor because of my mother's tenacity and strong will. For years, I saw my mother wear the same worn-down coat with a missing button. I knew my mother wanted more, but she put us first. Also, if she could have finished high school, she would have. But she had to stop to help her mother and father provide. My mother is one of the sole reasons I had to get a college education. I wanted to help my mother out far more than she could ever give me. She deserved nice things, and she deserved to retire and rest. I used that as motivation to further my education and attend Southern University in Baton Rouge.

In 1969, I graduated from W. H. Reed High School. W. H. Reed was the high school for Blacks. It was later integrated into Assumption High School post-segregation. My journey to college is different than most. Although I started in 1969, financial hardships hit back home. I had to take a step back and focus on how I could help my mother and family. So, I worked as a teacher's assistant in a reading laboratory at Napoleonville Primary School. From 1969-1972, I worked hard to help back home and save to continue my education. My mother was extremely vocal about me continuing my education because she didn't have the opportunity to choose. Again, I saw the things that shaped Louisiana, and I wanted to make a difference. Working in the reading laboratory ignited my flame to work with children.

I have always believed that equitable change begins in the community. A teacher named Dianne also encouraged me to go back to school and become a certified teacher. I had my mother's love, the motivation from a teacher, and the compassion for children driving me to go back to Southern University. Traveling to "Scott's Bluff" was completely different from living in Bertrandville. In the fall of 1972, I was only twenty years old. However, I was excited and eager to further my education and new beginnings. My sister, Lavern, was already attending school at the time. So, my freshman year, we were roommates along with Shirley, Barbara and Gilda. We rented a house off of Scenic Highway owned by a lady named Ms. Brown. Oh, how exciting it was to live in a larger community and "city" finally. I enjoyed my roommates dearly, and we all came from similar paths. On campus, I needed to find solid friendships with one common goal: to not only attend college, but to graduate!

Although grateful for housing, our home on Scenic Highway was a distance from campus! We literally had to walk everywhere because no one had a car. Lavern and I, and the others, would wake up around 5:30 A.M. every morning to prepare for class at 7:00 A.M.. It was effortless for me to engage and make new friends. It was within my freshman English class that I met my best friend still to this day, Linda Simms. The Simms sisters, Linda and Wanda, were my best friends. They lived in Alsen, which was a few miles outside of Baton Rouge. It was through them that I was able to network and meet even more people. I absolutely loved how the diversity within Black culture shaped the campus' essence, from our jargon and our style to the personal flair.

My mother would give me $25 to last a month, and boy, were we creative! Our survival mechanisms truly kicked in for food and entertainment. Even though we didn't have much, I was thrilled. I knew this sacrifice would lay the foundation for my future and the future of others. I was not a member of a Greek organization, but I was vocal and social. I always found myself engaging with students across various sectors of life and learning from others. That was the key! We were all family: the teachers, students and faculty. We all looked out for each other. We knew what it meant to survive, and we saw the greater outcome. The yard was filled with various social justice groups. We rallied, we organized, and we fought for change. We saw what a gift Southern University was to us, so we rallied to ensure that the university would remain for generations to come. We knew that the world was far more precious than campus life, but the vibes and culture on the yard were great. Southern University received visits from various folks, including Angela Davis, Muhammad Ali, Gladys Knight, and Marvin Gaye, and more!

Southern University taught me how important it was to embrace my culture and what it meant to stand out as a Black woman. Throughout the years, I found additional housing, and we even took some folks in. That's what it meant to be family and help others. One day, I met a young lady named Melba. She couldn't afford housing on campus, but she wanted an education. So, I spoke with my new roommates, and we took Melba into our apartment on Townsley Street. We saw the importance of sisterhood. We worked together to supply household items, food and even clothes. We were determined to help each other meet the finish line collectively.

The significance of creating a family-like bond and building relationships was more important than ever before my senior year. One of the main reasons for me completing college was to ensure that my mother never had to work as "the help" again. But I saw a stumbling block my senior year. My final class was with Dr. Stewart for student-teacher placement. I was so excited to have my last class and be closer to graduation, but I was the *only* female in the class. I then learned the importance of sharing my story, forming relationships, and what it meant to be family. What I initially viewed as a sense of inferiority, I viewed as my strength!

There is so much power in coming to your own and the strength of a Black woman. Although we varied in sex, I understood that my classmates and I were very much alike! We shared that same story of survival and growing up Black in America. We all wanted to go back home because folks depended on us! Family would not let family fail! So, we supported each other through each assignment. Upon completion of the class, Dr. Stewart didn't just view me as the only female. He saw me, a strong, intelligent Black woman with a goal to finish. At that very moment, I realized that Southern University would shape me for the rest of my life. SU taught me to work hard, remain humble, help others and never give up! I will always credit Southern University for giving me the best four years of my life. My graduation was bittersweet. My landlord, Mr. Right, ordered a cab for me on Townsley that day.

He said, "I will always view you as my daughter. So today, I don't want you to walk to campus. Today, you'll ride there in class." I can literally still see him as he stood outside and waved until the cab drove completely off. Once I graduated in December of 1976, my mother finally retired in January 1977! My mission and goal were complete. I was ready to take on the world!

Thank you, Southern University, for paving the way!

About Lucina Jamison

Lucina Heim Jamison is a proud native of Napoleonville, Louisiana, by way of Bertrandville. After graduating from W.H. Reed High School, she received her Bachelor of Art in Elementary Education from The Southern University and A&M College in 1970. Lucina attended Catholic School throughout her adolescent years, which attributes to her love and service in helping others. Throughout Assumption Parish, she is known for her connection to St. Benedict the Moor Catholic Church and St. Elizabeth School as she frequently volunteers and supports various programs for both organizations.

She is a proud member of St. Benedict the Moor's Inspirational Choir. For years, she dedicated her life as a 1st-grade school teacher at Labadieville Primary School. In her spare time, she enjoys the comfort of her family, sisters, and friends. She is a dedicated wife, mother and endearingly referred to as 'Nanny' throughout the community due to her love for mentoring children.

Christopher Levy

Live Gold Defend Blue
Christopher Levy

Hailing from the historic city of Donaldsonville, Louisiana, my connections to Southern University run deep. Donaldsonville natives include the first dean of the institution, John S. Jones, namesake to the storied freshmen men's dormitory, J. S. Jones Hall (aka Old Jones, demolished 2020) and father to Ralph Emerson Jones, second President of Grambling State University, and Governor Francis T. Nichols, who signed Act 87 into law, establishing Southern University in 1880. I discovered these little-known facts (post undergrad) through my quiet time and casual reading of Southern University history, coupled with my interest of general history. Donaldsonville is home to a host of Southern University graduates. Attending Southern is family tradition. I am one of many family members who have matriculated or is currently experiencing Scott's Bluff. My first introduction to Southern University was one summer traveling with my Tee Linda (SU Education '75) to drop of my cousin Lindsay (SU Engineering '05) who would be attending an SU summer enrichment program. I candidly remember crossing the hump and gasping as we passed Lacumba II, Southern's live jaguar. Little did I know, this summer trip would be the spark of my love affair with Southern University and A&M College.

As a freshman entering Southern in the fall of 2003, I was a grounded, yet lost eighteen-year-old. I was wondering and wandering in this new world of college life. Luckily, I had a few cousins on campus to help ensure I assimilated well. They spoiled me with trips to Walmart – trust me that was a privilege. Jones Hall was a rite of passage for men entering Southern University. This was my first time living out of my family home, and I cherished every moment. Jones Hall opened my eyes to a world outside of my normal small-town life I was accustomed to. The Res Life Circle during freshmen week was essentially Intro to Networking 101. This evening activity of hanging out in "The Circle" meeting new people was the beginning of my HBCU cultural experience. The Circle was a place where lifelong friends met. There was never a dull moment. Fall of 2003 was an overload of excellence, pride and tradition. Southern won the SWAC Football Championship, Pete Richardson's last as head coach. *College Hill* was in production, and the campus atmosphere was vibrant. Southern had lived up to the hype! On the bluff, I found pride. Pride that runs deep as the "river that flows onto the sea." Freshman semester truly confirmed that I had made the right choice in continuing the tradition of attending Southern University. Therefore, the journey began!

Coursework under my belt, I entered the College of Business (COB), majoring in marketing. The COB played a pivotal role in molding me into the service-driven leader I am today. It took a semester or so for me to engage with COB student organizations as a reserve student. Professor Katrice Albert encouraged others and me to sharpen our skills by way of the COB Marketing & Sales Club (COBMSC), COB Student Leadership Council (COBSLC), and other COB organizations. Before long, those words of encouragement resulted in me serving as Marketing & Sales Club Public Relations Manager, COBSLC Homecoming Committee Co-Chair, and Black Executive Exchange Program (BEEP) Vice President. These leadership roles presented opportunities to create the first marketing and sales conference; personally invite business executives to visit and become mentors; organize the BEEP Career Awareness and Planning Seminar; and lend my creativity to the homecoming committee – conceptualizing Mr. and Miss College of Business. Through student organizations, I met four lifelong friends who I will forever share a bond with: Antoria, Kim, Anthony. We dubbed ourselves the COB Fab 4. Representing and serving the College of Business and its students was a pleasure. My passion to serve and preserve Southern University was cultivated in the halls of T.T. Allain.

While my calendar was full of COB classes and activities, I also worked full time at Albertsons. Albertsons was my first job in high school. Now, I was the Assistant Front End Manager. If it were not for my HBCU, and its village of support that continued to pour life into me through my challenges, or Ms. Albert's continuously demanding excellence, I would not be the driven, well-rounded professional I am today. Balancing school, work and life was most definitely a struggle. But it was necessary in my development as a leader and an advocate of HBCU students.

On December 12, 2008, I became alumnus of the Southern University and A&M College. However, my work to preserve its legacy was just beginning. By March of 2009, I decided to move and settled in Dallas, Texas. Dallas, unbeknownst to me, was home to hundreds of Jaguars and a highly active alumni chapter. Joining the Dallas alumni chapter afforded me the chance to rub shoulders with Southernites who were movers and shakers in the DFW Metroplex. I appreciated the longevity and excellence of Southern, and further honed my leadership skills. As I volunteered and learned the functions of the alumni chapter, I was charged with helping the chapter engage and invite young alumni. Chapter President LaQuitta Thomas appointed me co-chair of the newly formed Y2K Jags committee with the charge in mind. Our committee created the chapter's first day party series, Dallas Jags Connect, in an effort to provide a space for DFW area Southernites, young and seasoned, to chat, connect and celebrate being a Jaguar. While a member of the Dallas chapter, I served on the student relations committee, Bayou Bash committee (chapter annual crawfish bowl fundraiser 35+ years), Founders Golf Tournament committee, and second vice president/ membership committee chair. Serving as an alumni recruiter helped me connect my passion, Southern University, and my purpose, student advocacy. Conversing with young adults regarding career goals, and the Southern University experience, became second nature. This is a testament to the knowledge of Southern University, and college and career readiness.

After living in Dallas ten years, I returned to Louisiana and Southern University with passion and purpose in tow. Today, as an employee of the university, I am influencing and transforming lives daily. Serving as the university scholarship counselor, my goal is to assist students with maximizing all resources and engaging as many with alumni mentors. Currently, I continue to persevere the legacy of Southern through the Southern University Alumni Federation (SUAF). I was appointed Southern University Young Alumni

Network (SUYAN) – National Chairman. SUYAN works to engage and recognize the achievements of young alumni, while increasing the membership and programs of SUAF. Servicing Southern and the Jaguar Nation started as a passion, but I am convinced it is my purpose.

Our alma mater states, "We owe our all to thee!" I most certainly do.

About Christopher M. Levy

Christopher M. Levy is a native of Donaldsonville, La. He is a fall 2008 graduate of the College of Business at Southern University with a B.S. in Marketing - Professional Sales.

Christopher resides in Denham Springs, LA and currently serves as the Scholarship Counselor at Southern University and A&M College. Through his role, Christopher educates minority, first generation, & undeserved students on the financial aid process and resources available for college, motivates students through their matriculation, and advocates on students behave. Christopher prides himself on ensuring the best student experience.

Christopher is a life member of the Southern University Alumni Federation (SUAF) where he is in his second term as Southern University Young Alumni Network (SUYAN) National Chairman. As National Chairman, he leads a team of young alumni in developing engagement programs geared toward increasing membership of SUAF. Under his leadership, SUYAN has worked to cultivate a culture of philanthropy, reached 1500 paid alumni members under the age of 40, expanded its footprint to ten SUAF chapter cities, and now manages the SUAF 40 Under Forty awards.

Christopher spends his spare time cooking, traveling, and recruiting for Southern University.

Kimberlee Collins-Walker

Three Things I Learned at Southern U.
Kimberlee Collins-Walker

I grew up around the Southern University community. We listened to The Human Jukebox in our backyards as they practiced for parades, games or festivals. I also attended Southern University sporting events with my family. The Southern University culture is very different. In the south, you find that southern accent, first-class hospitality and delicious cuisine. The music is amazing, and it is a totally different culture.

Upon registering for school, I needed to pick a major that was recession-proof. I knew I wanted a career in the business world, but I was torn between business management or accounting. It was a Southern University alumna who introduced me to the world of accounting. I was admitted to other schools that were not HBCUs, but it was the Southern University culture, and my high school mentor, who guided my decision to attend "The Great Southern University". Also, I wanted my college education to be where mainly minority students made up majority of the student population. My first day at freshman registration, I was excited to be "officially" the driver to my educational journey. Little did I know, I was in for the ride of my life. During my freshman orientation, the advisor said, "There is a possibility that the friends you start your freshman year in college with will not be with you to end your senior year and graduate with. They will get caught up in the college party life and life will happen. Don't let that be you."

I assumed that statement wasn't true, until my second semester of my sophomore year. I found myself oversleeping, missing classes, partying and doing all the things my advisor warned me about. My sophomore year at Southern University was tough, but I had a lot to learn quickly. College is totally different from high school. My professors had a higher level of expectations for me. My experience at Southern University prepared me for the "real world" and, as an African American woman in a predominately "White male" field of accounting, I knew I would have to put in the extra work.

Three things I learned while I was a student at Southern

University are the spirit of patience, the power of knowledge and the courage to network.

The Spirit of Patience

I learned the spirit of patience early my freshman year. The registration process was very seldom a smooth process, no matter how much I prepared to get the information on time. Every higher education institution has its ups and downs. You must learn how to work through the difficulties. But when you finish a registration process at Southern University, you are able to conquer the world. Of course, times and technology have changed. But, during my era, they were just starting to integrate the online registration process. It had hiccups, to say the least. I learned that everything will not always go your way, no matter how much you prepare. Things will happen. Over the years, I learned to have patience and leave it to the higher power to work it out. Having patience doesn't mean I took "No" for an answer. But it taught me how to deal with complications and create new ways to handle mishaps.

The Power of Knowledge

I wanted to go to college to seek post-secondary education. But I learned so much more at Southern University. I learned more about my African American culture that I was not taught in elementary or secondary education. I learned about the positive impacts of our ancestors and our culture, which was embedded all over campus. In my classes, I was taught how the African American culture contributed to everything. I walked away knowing the positive history of my culture and having the confidence to know that anything is possible if I just stay focused.

The Courage to Network

My junior year at Southern University, I was asked to participate in our annual career fair. I was extremely nervous. I just knew my resume would get me the internship I was looking for, but I was wrong. It was my career services advisor and accounting professor who informed me that networking is key and being shy will keep me jobless. After that harsh reality, I started attending networking workshops provided by Career Services.

At Southern University, we had a day called "Pretty Wednesday." I used this day to dress up and network at the union. Sometimes, it was serious networking. Other times, it was just for fun. But this experience definitely helped me with my networking skills. I learned quickly that it is not always what you know, but who you know and who knows you.

During my years at Southern University, I learned the value of maintaining good relationships with whomever I met. I quickly got over my shyness and started networking with various students, professors and visitors all over campus. During my junior year, I reached out to Dr. Cathy Hardnett-McCaloupe, who was an adjunct professor at Southern University. I expressed my interest in gaining experience in the accounting field. She owned a CPA firm in Baton Rouge, and she gave me the opportunity to learn the public side of accounting. I had other opportunities to gain accounting experience in the government side of accounting, but I wanted to learn from a SU alumna who was an entrepreneur. My networking with her allowed me to become a partner at her firm in 2011. This was one of the best opportunities I ever encountered. Even with her untimely death in 2012, I remained a partner at the firm until 2014.

I am forever grateful to the Southern University faculty and staff for helping to mold me into the individual I am today. I will always say my *SUccess* came from God, my parents and Southern University A&M College. I did not just earn a degree from Southern University. I learned lessons about myself and my culture.

About Kimberlee Collins-Walker

Kimberlee Collins-Walker is the owner of Assurance Tax and Accounting Group (ATAG), a full- service tax and accounting firm and Pinkins Medical Transportation (PMT), a medical transportation company, Kimberlee is no stranger to hard work and entrepreneurship. A graduate of Southern University and A&M College (Baton Rouge) Bachelor of Science - Accounting. Kimberlee is dedicated to empowering businesses to maximize their efforts by building a business that not only makes money, but also builds wealth. Kimberlee prides herself on taking her clients' ill feelings towards income tax and helping them achieve a happy and healthy outcome on income tax reduction and management.

A native of Baton Rouge, LA, Kimberlee is the Treasurer of the Southern University Alumni Home Chapter, an active member of Sigma Gamma Rho Sorority and St. Paul Missionary Baptist Church. Mrs. Walker has been featured in Beautiful Black magazine, The Rouge Collection, WAFB, Nola.com, Cumulus Radio and her very own Facebook Live "Ask the Tax Doctor" a question and answer series.

She is the wife of Mark Walker and the parents of Collin Pinkins-Walker & Mikayla Walker. During football season, you can find them the stands supporting their favorite teams the Southern University Jaguars and the New Orleans Saints.

Alaric Jones

Made by the Bluff, Raised by the Bluff, Paid by the Bluff

Alaric Jones

The majority of my HBCU college experience came from the Bluffs of the Mississippi River at Southern University. My experiences at SU helped mold me into the person I am today. I credit all aspects of my HBCU to contributing to my experience like friends, academics, Greek life, networking and tradition.

I started at Southern University, or "The Bluff", in 2010; however, my SU experience started well before I arrived on campus. Being a third-generation jaguar, my family was always influential in my SU experience. My grandmother graduated from SU in 1967. My mom, a social work major from Alexandria, Louisiana, graduated from SU. My dad, a math major from New Orleans, also attended SU. In the late 1980s, these two met on the yard between Jones and Boley Hall during a math tutoring session. After having their own HBCU love experience, I was born a few years later. I would not be here if it wasn't for Southern University.

Growing up in Louisiana, most Blacks have some ties to the HBCUs in the state. Many people have family members who either went to Southern or Grambling. Household rivalries may split families during the Bayou Classic. Growing up, my mother always had me immersed in the jaguar spirit. We headed to Baton Rouge every year to catch a game or two. Every year, I was excited for the Bayou Classic, whether I watched it on TV or I was there in person. The atmosphere of SU games always excited me because the band was jamming, the crowd was cheering, and the football team was scoring. My favorite sport is baseball, so I was also able to watch the SU baseball team win conference championships while I was younger. SU grad, Rickie Weeks, who became one of my favorite MLB players, was the Golden Spikes award winner (Player of the Year in all of College) and was drafted #2 overall by the Milwaukee Brewers in 2003. He was one of my idols growing up. My experiences as a kid contributed to my jaguar spirit today.

Coupled with my family being SU alums, and my experiences as a kid, I decided to attend SU. I started in the summer of 2010 so I could get a head start and get acclimated to campus before the fall. I was a part of the Timbuktu program, which helped pay my tuition that summer. The Timbuktu program helps minorities in STEM majors complete research. My freshman year at SU was an incredibly fun experience. My roommate was my best friend, so we did everything together. We had the same major, so we literally studied, ate and partied together. We always held each other accountable when one of us was slipping.

I was a chemistry major at SU. I was always interested in math and chemistry in high school. However, this was not an easy major while studying this in college. Some classes seemed like I was taking a foreign language. Many days, I felt defeated by the coursework. As an outgoing person, I spent a lot of time hanging out at the union rather than studying. I had to learn to prioritize. I was also blessed to have some great chemistry professors at SU, like the late Dr. Moore (the first Black Ph.D. recipient from Purdue), Dr. Jones, and Dr. Whicker (Kentucky State University's current College of Science department head). Dr. Whicker probably had the most impact on me and all my classmates. He pushed us so hard to be prepared for the real world in chemistry. He expected our lab reports to be detailed and we had to be on point when doing lab experiments. To make sure we understood the material, his tests were always in essay form. That way, we could articulate our learnings and findings. Sometimes, as Black people in STEM, we have a hard time presenting our findings. This helped us in that aspect. Today, I keep that same work ethic on the job that he taught us. It has contributed greatly to the success in my career.

During my time at my HBCU, I was able to do four internships. SU and PV did a great job of exposing its students to large companies to gain experiences, whether it was via internships or full-time jobs. I was able to intern with Shell (Houston, TX), GE Aviation (Cincinnati, OH), Nucor Steel (Convent, LA), and Monsanto (St. Louis, MO). Both of my HBCUs prepared me for the work environment by exposing me to real-world applications and preparing us for interviews. The classes I took at PV in my master's program help me greatly on my job today. Dr. Reeves was known as the toughest teacher in the chemical engineering department, but I loved her because she presented a challenge in the coursework she taught.

Today, I work as a process engineer for an oil and gas company. I support a chemical process unit in Houston and another in Gelsenkirchen, Germany. In my current role, I have worked with engineers from top engineering schools like Michigan, University of Texas, MIT, and many more. When working with my peers, my work has always been above and beyond others. In some cases, I must manage others from these schools. I credit my HBCU experiences for preparing me to handle the work environment where you might not necessarily come from the "best" school.

My first two semesters, I was able to get acclimated to the yard and see how things went. During this time, I was able to see Greek life for the first time also. I really didn't have any family members who were Greek, but my mom always told me my dad had friends that were Omegas. Once I got to school, I was able to see how they interacted up close and I was quickly interested in joining the organization. I quickly showed my interest to one of the current members at the time because we took Calculus together. Somehow, I ended up helping him on some homework and tests. I was able to be initiated into the Beta Sigma Chapter at Southern University in the fall of 2011. My time on campus as an Omega was an exceptionally good time. I was able to win step shows in front of 40,000 people at the Bayou Classic. I've been able to network with famous people and earn an internship through the fraternity from GE. As the International Undergraduate Representative of Omega Psi Phi, I was over all undergraduate members worldwide. In this position, I was able to meet many talented undergraduate brothers. I was also able to travel the country in this capacity to speak to brothers. During this time, I was able to present Muhammed Ali with a lifetime achievement award right before he passed. In this position, when speaking to brothers, I always talked about my HBCU and the experiences I had on the yard to those who didn't have an HBCU experience. Many of the brothers who didn't get that HBCU experience have gone on to get master's degrees from

HBCUs due to our conversations.

Overall, my SU experience molded me into the person I am today. From the time my parents met, the SU experience has been making a lasting impact on my life. I try to share the things I experienced at my HBCU with others so that they are able to have a similar experience to mine. A combination of friends, academics, Greek life, and many other things have made my HBCU experiences one that I will remember for the rest of my life. "The Bluff" will always have a place in my heart.

Geaux Jags!

About Alaric Jones

"Alaric hails from the great city of Alexandria, Louisiana where he attended Peabody Magnet High School. He is a graduate of Southern University and A&M College, in Baton Rouge, Louisiana, where he received his B.S. in Chemistry. He also received his M.S. in Chemical Engineering from Prairie View A&M University, in Praire View, Texas.

Alaric currently lives in the city of Houston, TX, where he works as Process Engineer in the oil and gas industry. Alaric is a member of the Southern University Alumni Association-Houston Chapter. He also gives back to his university by being a season ticket holder for the football and baseball teams. He was initiated into the Beta Sigma Chapter of Omega Psi Phi Fraternity, Inc. at Southern University. In his fraternity, he held the position of International Undergraduate Representative to the Supreme Council. He gives back in the city of Houston by helping increase the participation of African American youth in the sport of baseball by mentoring and hosting camps. Along with sports, he also volunteers to help promote STEM (Science, Technology, Engineering, and Math) among African American youth. Alaric loves to watch sports and is an avid Southern University and Saints fan! #GeauxJags #WhoDat"

Ayanna Spivey

A Royal Alignment

Ayanna Spivey

Attending Southern University, truly taught me that going with your first mind is almost always the best decision. Growing up with two parents and a grandmother who are all proud Southernites, I watched the Bayou Classic in my living room every year. My grandmother sent my brother and I Southern gear just to wear in our living room. By the time my senior year came around, I had applied to Southern, of course. But I did have my eyes set on in-state schools like California State University, East Bay and Tuskegee University. My mother decided it was time for her to step in. She finally took us to the Bayou Classic so I could see it live and in living color. Honestly, it was an easy sell. Once I saw all of the Black people, the Greeks and the bands, I was hooked. There was so much of a familial atmosphere that it felt like home already. I was reacquainted with my mom's good college friends, who happened to be my brother's godparents. With my grandmother only being about an hour away in Bogalusa, Louisiana, it was obviously the right decision. After turning down nine acceptances to other colleges and giving up scholarships and grants, two days after my eighteenth birthday my mother sent me off to the Bluff.

My time at Southern University was truly a whirlwind of experiences. As a freshman it was surreal being an actual student there and being amongst the Human Jukebox, Dancing Dolls, and the royal court as my classmates. It was so astonishing to me. However, aside from the astonishment, I did come on campus with a plan: to graduate and become a member of Delta Sigma Theta Sorority, Inc. That was it. However, I did not know what the journey was going to look like. I started my matriculation by getting actively involved in the student government association (SGA) as a freshman class senator. I was able to see first-hand how homecoming and other events came together on campus. If I didn't know before that Southern was for me, that first homecoming proved just that. Homecoming events, organizational pageants, the BET Black College Tour, and awareness weeks, reminded me that I wanted to continue to be a part of the process in making these things happen. I wanted to run for a leadership position. What suited me best at the time was Miss Sophomore. Plus, I had friends who were already going to run for sophomore class president and vice president.

Running for a queen position at Southern drastically challenged the person I thought I was and how I presented myself. I was relatively a tomboy. I was rough around the edges my entire life. I wasn't into makeup, dresses, and especially not tiaras. So, it surely perplexed my mother when I presented the idea to her. However, my understanding of the position was that it would allow me a key position at the table in planning the events for my class and the university ultimately, while supporting the endeavors of Miss Southern University. That sounded easy enough. I'd held positons in high school and on the regional level. I had the ability already to speak well and speak in front of crowds. I went for it.

HBCU spring campaign season is a big deal. But Southern is on *another* level. The energy can be defined as electric; the air is rare. The college never sleeps. Candidates go all out with their themes, materials and giveaways. Southern's campaign season has a history of plane flyovers, McDonald's breakfast every morning, and groundbreaking Miss Southern talent performances. Coming into this was a bit intimidating. I could only imagine how much the campaigns cost and the thought process went into all the creativity of these campaigns. I struggled if I could live up to the prestige. Nonetheless I scrambled up my friends and available resources to run. Luckily, I came out victorious.

Becoming Miss Sophomore opened the door to several opportunities that I could have never imagined. These occurrences included being a part of the new student orientation program and assisting the football team with their on-campus recruitment visits. It was especially awe-inspiring to be one of the first people future Jaguars would meet. I loved introducing them to the Southern University I was finally able to really know, separate from my parents' and grandmother's experiences. One of the most satisfying opportunities to come from my time as Miss Sophomore, was knocking off one of two of my original goals: becoming a member of the Alpha Tau Chapter of Delta Sigma Theta Sorority, Inc. That journey was beyond words. It was not an easy one; but it was fulfilling. I do not have any biological sisters, nor did I grow up around many female cousins who were my age. So being a part of this global sisterhood was more than gratifying. However, it was bittersweet since my family were unable to attend. As we finished presenting ourselves to the campus as the new initiates, all of my line sisters were being rushed by their family and friends, I stood there alone. I will never forget that small moment. Soon after, my god sisters found me, and my friends followed right after. It was an overflow of tears and love. Being 2,000 miles away from home is never easy, especially when you're in an entirely new environment. I knew then, I had found my tribe and place of being at Southern.

That place of being led me to the outrageous idea of running for Miss Southern University. I used all my resources and some even fell in my lap in pursuing this esteemed title and position. My sorority sisters Airee and Kenya came together to assist with my campaign theme, talent choreography and a last-minute pageant gown. My friend, Justin, surprised me with a campaign song and my other friend Garrett offered to shoot a video for it. The culmination of the known and unknown support made this once outrageous idea a reality as I was bestowed the title of the 83rd Miss Southern University and A&M College. One of the main two things I wanted to accomplish as queen was to raise awareness and funds for agencies that supported sickle cell and kidney disease. As these are two major epidemics in the Black community. It was especially personal to me as my mother lived with a rare kidney disease. Along with those philanthropic endeavors, I wanted to elevate my college's notoriety on a national scale. Also, my time as Miss Southern encompassed a series of major events. I was asked to be the trophy girl for the McDonald's 365 Black Awards that aired on BET of August 2013. I was able to return to the NASAP Student Leadership Institute (SLI), which allowed me to expand my HBCU network outside of the Southwest Athletic Conference (SWAC). I was the first Miss Southern to be a part of the Top 10 Ebony HBCU Campus Queens. I was able to grace the front page of the Baton Rouge Advocate newspaper during homecoming, which is rare because that year we shared our homecoming weekend with LSU. I represented the institution in a national commercial that aired during the Bayou Classic and the SWAC championship. I traveled back to my home state to recruit at one of the largest HBCU college fairs in Los Angeles, Ca. Words cannot express the magnitude of representing Southern University during that year.

Not only did Southern provide me with various chances to expand my leadership skills and find new ones, but it also provided me occasions to be in rooms with cultural icons such as Reverend Jesse Jackson, Minister Louis Farrakhan, Sister Soulja, the late Representative John Lewis, and the late John Singleton. All these significant events made for a remarkable four years at my beloved Southern University. Although, I started this journey unsure of what it would like, or how I would even get there. I accomplished my goals and then some. My time as a Jaguar showed me the power of alignment. Each moment, each accomplishment, each obstacle all came together to help me reach my goals. It allowed me to understand the power in my network and my tribe. I have gained some life-long friends and the godparents to my future children. I had the opportunity to build and expand on the foundation I already had. My matriculation in and out of the classroom set a precedent for my career in higher education and student services. 'Til this day, I always say I could have graduated and became a Delta at any university. But I could not have done it the way, and/or on the scale, that I did at Southern University and A&M College. For that, I am forever grateful.

About Ayanna Spivey

Ayanna Spivey was born in the shadow of Southern University in Baton Rouge, LA. She was raised in Moreno Valley, Ca. Ayanna's leadership skills and creativity revealed themselves early in her childhood from being involved in her home church's youth ministry, youth choir, youth council, and various social events. She really explored those skills while in high school lettering in 3 sports, active in Associated Student Body, Black Student Union, and the becoming the Southern California Regional President of Black Student Unions. These experiences laid the foundation for her time at Southern University and the beginning of her career in higher education, through various positions in the Student Government Association, Miss Sophomore and then Miss Southern on the Royal Court. She also took part in the new student summer orientations, football recruiting, and being a member of the Alpha Tau chapter of Delta Sigma Theta Sorority Inc. All these endeavors sparked the ideas of wanting to go into higher education. Upon graduating from Southern University with a Bachelors Degree in Interdisciplinary Studies, with a concentration in Social Work and Sociology, she returned to California and received a Master of Science in Higher Education leadership andStudent Development from California Baptist University.

With the culmination of her secondary and post-secondary education, in 2016 she launched We Are Educated, LLC. We Are Educated, LLC is an organization that strives to promote higher learning at HBCUs and inspire academic excellence through college preparation. It is the organization's belief that it can play a part in the increase of HBCU attendance by highlighting the benefits of the overall HBCU experience. We Are Educated, LLC provides scholarships to assist undergraduate students with their matriculation through various workshops and fairs. We Are Educated, LLC has provided about $3000 plus in giving within its first two years. We Are Educated, is currently going through a rebranding transformation, and is in the process of becoming an official nonprofit tax exempt company and will be relaunching summer of 2021.

Since her career path continued in California, Ayanna has worked within the California Community College system going on 7 years working with various programs that includes academic counseling, student services, academic success programs and with the California Department of Corrections and Rehabilitation. Her passions for equity and student success are evident in the work that she does within her perspective departments by always putting the students and their interests first. It is her hope to continue within the community college system while also contemplating on the idea of pursuing a doctoral degree. In the meantime, she continues to be active with the Southern University Alumni Federation Alumni Los Angeles Chapter, Southern University Young Alumni Network and she was named as one of SU's 40 Under Forty for the inaugural cohort in 2018.

Joseph Robins

A Jaguar's Journey
Joseph Robins

Being born and raised in Baton Rouge, Louisiana, by family and friends who are Southern University and A&M College alumni, I had no choice but to be engulfed in the culture of the Jaguar Nation at an early age. I remember attending numerous events and being involved in various school-related programs on campus that not only helped me develop as an adolescent, but also fostered my love for the university and everything it had to offer. I began my college experience in the fall of 2009 as a crab in the world-renowned Human Jukebox Marching Band. As an eighteen-year-old freshman on a college campus, this was one of the first families I was a part of. But it certainly wasn't the last. Being a member of The Jukebox taught me the importance of time management. We practiced for countless hours during the weekday, while also having to maintain our course load. Not only did the marching band teach me time management, but it also helped promote my ability to work in a team. People asked me all the time how a 200-member organization was able to execute a flawless performance during halftime every week. My response was always, "Teamwork makes the dream work." Of course, there was a plethora of varying personalities, character traits, attitudes, demographics and ways of thinking. But, in order to operate in excellence, we had to execute as one cohesive unit.

The skills I learned while being a member of such a large organization for four years transcended into not only me being involved in other organizations on campus, but also my professional career, as well. As I matriculated through college, I engulfed myself in various organizations including the Black Executive Exchange Program and Pi Sigma Epsilon Professional Sales and Marketing Fraternity. Through my various affiliations, I made friendships and connections with people, which I still maintain today. Upon entering my senior year, I gained the distinct privilege of becoming a member of the Beta Sigma Chapter of Omega Psi Phi Fraternity, Incorporated. I was elected Basileus of the chapter after we crossed. This position required me to utilize all the skills I learned during college! Having to navigate between family, work, fraternity responsibilities, contact with administration, and trying to graduate was quite the hassle. But, as a chapter, we made it happen! During my tenure, we won the 2013 Homecoming Greek Show and Bayou Classic Greek Show. We were voted Favorite Fraternity, participated in countless community service projects, graduated all the brothers in the chapter, and hosted the *best* parties and tailgates the yard had to offer (not up for debate). My life at Southern University was the culmination of varying opportunities, failures, successes, mistakes, relationships and lessons. I honestly would not change any aspect of my life as an undergrad. Every instance served its purpose.

Love

When I began my college experience, I had this weird expectation that I needed to find my wife before I graduate, or else I would be single for the rest of my life. Ironically, I began dating my wife before I graduated (literally the semester of my graduation). But I wouldn't say that should be your thought process as you go throughout your college career. One weekend during my junior year, I went to the club with a few friends and saw her dancing. My wife is from New Orleans. Let's just say how she was moving to the bounce music had me mesmerized. I had to get her. I ended up getting her number that night, but it felt like every time I reached out to her, she never responded to me, at least not directly. She always texted me in a random group message with strangers, inviting me to events on campus.

I attended one of the events and tried to talk to her, but she did not give me the time of day. This made me feel like she wasn't really interested in me. It was as if she had just given me her number to promote her campus events. I stopped pursuing her at this point. However, every so often, she would randomly go on a picture liking spree via my Instagram page. As millennials, we know that this could mean a person is interested in you. At this point, I figured she was crazy. But I was crazy, too. So, I liked all of her pictures right back. This went on for months, and neither of us would make a move. One faithful night, she sent me a random text message, expressing her affection toward me. She told me she was always so nervous to talk to me directly. I immediately responded that I was interested in her, as well. However, at the time I was pursuing membership into my fraternity. So, I didn't really have a lot of time on my hands. I ultimately dropped the ball on maintaining communication. After we crossed, we had this big party, and she came to find me. Ironically, I was looking for her, as well. We exchanged numbers again and kept in contact over the summer up until the following fall semester. That fall semester, I messed up the whole situation and had to work pretty hard to get back in the mix. We both ended up attending the Thurgood Marshall Leadership Conference that fall. At that point, I knew it was all or nothing. I spent the whole trip pursuing her. She ended up giving in and allowing me another shot! From that point, we dated for the next five years. We married in August of 2019. We both realize that, had it not been for our dear university, we don't know if we would have ever met.

Legacy

Initially, I thought if I marched in the band, and made good grades, I would get a job after college and be successful. Boy was I completely wrong. My freshman and sophomore year, I worked a part-time job, marched in the band, and maintained my grades. My junior year, I was afforded the opportunity to interview for a summer internship in Houston. I had a phenomenal on-campus interview. But when I flew to Houston for the on-site interview, I realized how ill-prepared I was compared to the competition. It was this point in my college experience that I realized I needed to invest more time in my professional development. I joined the Black Executive Exchange Program (BEEP) that semester and gained real-world insight from peers who had various internship and leadership opportunities in the workforce. This organization gave me the impromptu speaking, resume writing, interviewing and other professional skills necessary to make it.

I later joined Pi Sigma Epsilon Professional Sales and Marketing Fraternity, which helped polish the skills I learned in BEEP. Joining those organizations was a turning point for me. The following summer, I was afforded the opportunity to study abroad in London, England. My classmates and I were the only students from an HBCU campus, but we definitely left our mark on the program. That excursion opened doors for me going into my senior year. I was blessed with the opportunity to intern on Wall Street for the summer. Living in Manhattan and being immersed in the financial services industry shed light on how far behind we were in my community regarding financial services. I vowed to utilize the information I learned to help improve and influence my people. I vowed to be the change I want to see!

I graduated with Latin Honors and Chief Marshall of the College of Business in 2014. Upon graduation, I gained employment at a public accounting firm and, in 2015, became a licensed Certified Public Accountant, making me the youngest black CPA at the firm. In 2017, I decided to branch out and start my own practice, J. Robins CPA, LLC. In conjunction with starting my practice, I also acquired my FINRA Series 7 and Series 66 licenses and became a financial advisor with Equitable Advisors. I have utilized these platforms over the past few years to provide quality, legal and accurate financial services to an underserved community. My goal is to connect with serious individuals who are looking to build, maintain and transfer wealth across generations and ultimately change the financial landscape for Black and brown individuals in America. If not for relationships made, lessons learned, and opportunities gained at Southern, I do not know where I would be. I can honestly say that much of my way of thinking was shaped by the experiences afforded me through my HBCU.

I will be forever grateful!

About Joseph Robins

Joseph Robins is a native of Baton Rouge, Louisiana, a 2009 graduate of Scotlandville Magnet High School, and a 2014 graduate of the College of Business at Southern University and A&M College. While at Southern, Joseph was actively involved in various organizations such as BEEP, Pi Sigma Epsilon, Beta Gamma Sigma, the College of Business Student Leadership Council, a four-year member of the Southern University "Human JukeBoxx" Marching Band, and a Spring 2013 initiate of the Beta Sigma Chapter of Omega Psi Phi Fraternity Incorporated. Joseph graduated as Chief Marshall of the College of Business with Latin Honors and dual degrees in Accounting and Finance. Upon graduation Joseph received full time employment as a staff auditor at a local accounting firm. While employed at firm Joseph obtained a significant amount of knowledge in regard to audit and assurance services and was also able to pass all four required sections of the Certified Public Accounting Examination. Joseph was officially licensed in December of 2015 making him the youngest practicing African American CPA at the firm. In 2017 Joseph decided to leave the firm and start a new career as a dual professional in the financial services industry. Joseph is currently the Owner/President of J.Robins CPA, LLC and is also a FINRA licensed Financial Professional with Equitable Advisors. Within these roles Joseph provides small business bookkeeping/accounting, business consultation, individual/business tax planning and preparation, retirement planning, investment planning, and insurance planning. In recognition for his achievements, Joseph was inducted into the Southern University Alumni Federation 40 under 40 inaugural cohorts in 2018! Joseph also currently serves as a Senior Vice President and Affiliate Owner of the Florida Territory for Global Tax Centers Inc. and Is also the Vice President of OLU Investments Inc. As he continues to grow his practice and influence Joseph plans to use his various platforms to continue providing sound financial advice and services to clients and aims to positively impact the daily lives of the people in his community through his leadership and good works.

Ja'el Gordon

The Ancestors are Shining Upon Us
Ja'el Gordon

While there are several traditional and cultural reasons I chose to attend Southern University and A&M College Baton Rouge, the main reason for my choice was to pay homage and honor those who were enslaved on the lands prior to the establishment of the university. I could have chosen any university or HBCU; however, it was seeing the Archives Building as a kid that drew me in, and I wanted to learn more. At the time, my mother was a student in the School of Nursing, and she worked in the Law Center. We always passed that white building. I envisioned that, one day, I would be able to tell its story. After learning that the university's land once housed a plantation of which the building stood and operated on, I wanted to learn about the many enslaved people who were legally disenfranchised, treated as movable property, and legally prohibited from obtaining an education. At an early age, I decided that that is where I wanted to work. I wanted to be able to preserve the history of those who came before us and the history of the institution. It was preservation for those who cultivated the lands for which Southern University was able to purchase and establish a great institution upon. I wanted to learn more about the struggles and triumphs our dear founders had when they made the decision to make this spot the home of the Jaguars. Southern University was able to provide what our ancestors could not: a rightful education.

I also learned as a child roaming the campus the history of the Smith-Brown murders. I could not fathom how and why such an incident could happen in such a sacred space. This was "our" space that was to be protected and revered. After learning that the students who were protesting that fateful day on the campus did so because they wanted better education, and wanted change, that solidified my decision to attend Southern University. We, as a people, have fought for hundreds of years to be heard and to have rights. So, I needed to continue that legacy of going to this HBCU so that none of that would be in vain. It became my dream and drive to learn as much as I could about the history and culture of the university in order to preserve it for future generations. I wanted to be able to experience what my ancestors could not, but also give them a voice to never be forgotten. Why would I not go to such an institution that made a sacrifice to build a pathway for someone that looks like me when no others would?

I enrolled in the great Southern University in 1999. I became obsessed with gaining as much knowledge and experience about HBCU culture as I possibly could. This was literally the age of the living LaCumba, whom I was in awe of. How many institutions can say they've had a live mascot? I was intrigued! I did not have the "Different World" expectations when I enrolled, and it did not have any bearing on my decision. I wasn't expecting the Black Power Movement either. But what I did expect was to be embraced and accepted—not by trauma bonding—but of culture and by common likeness of being amazing people who survived and finally got the recognition they deserve. It was the important, yet simple, fact that I felt I owed my success to those who did not have the same opportunity. The history of this institution alone deserves so much recognition for paving the way for so many scholars who otherwise would not have the opportunity to become one. The unfortunate, yet fortunate, thing is that I decided to leave after a year and a half.

I suffered extremely from social anxiety, which prevented me from fully enjoying or embracing my opportunity. After leaving the institution for a few years to go in the workforce, it dawned on me in 2007 that I needed to fulfill that dream and gain the knowledge that was rightfully mine in this historical institution. It was then that I decided to embark on my full journey of becoming a scholar of history. I was already doing genealogy work. So, the historian route not only paid homage to those who worked the lands and those who enrolled in the early establishment of the institution, but also for the preservation of our story for future generations. I told myself that I could do this. I owed it to myself to finish what I dreamed of. Our ancestors were not fearful. The first graduating class of the institution's J.S. Clark was not fearful. The students protesting during the Smith-Brown murders were not fearful. They knew risk. They knew they had a voice, and they could pave the way for others by showing up. It is a dishonor to not carry that same esteem and confidence. Luckily, I was able to further develop myself in so many areas after I re-enrolled in 2007.

Wanting to become more involved on an interactional level, I decided to step out on a leap of faith by getting involved with the Student Government Association. It was a decision that changed my life. It was one of the greatest decisions I made. I had the opportunity to meet so many like-minded students and not-so-like minded students, community partners and administrators. It helped me gain confidence of my own ability. I realized I had a place in the world, and I had a voice. Always being a creative-minded innovator and a person who loves to help others, it was easy for me to assess the needs of my fellow peers, even if I was considered a non-traditional student. I had the opportunity to serve as the Association for Women Students' President for two terms, something I honestly feel I would not have had the opportunity to do if I had gone to a predominantly white institution. I wholeheartedly believe that an education is an education, no matter what institution a person chooses. However, it is the wholistic nurturing that an HBCU provides in navigating through a world of uncertainties that I needed.

I was scheduled to graduate in 2011. However, the death of my mother hindered this possibility. In the back of my mind, I knew I had to still make her proud, by any means necessary, through diligence and determination. I could not again leave the place I loved and the place she loved so very much. I had to do something. This university and the community deserved the same love and encouragement that I had received for so many years. After having heart-to-heart conversations with my professors, I lessened my course load, which in turn gave me the opportunity to dig deeper into the needs of those around me. Knowing my graduation was postponed until 2012, I had time to work on finding ways to assist in providing Black students with an opportunity of pride of obtaining an education.

Southern University helped me through my ups and downs. It helped me become a better, more engaged person. Southern was patient with me when I was not patient with myself. It gave me opportunity and selfless purpose. This sentiment allowed my then

SGA President and me to birth the Office of Student Organizations, to which I served as coordinator of for many years. Students needed voices. They needed a drive. They needed someone to believe in them. But they also needed someone to instill in them the importance of not taking anything or any freedoms for granted. We have a rightful place in this world. Just as Southern gave a platform to so many before me, I wanted them to know they were afforded the same. I wanted the student body to have the opportunity to have the full Black experience outside of merely having the HBCU association. Black culture and Black life mean the world to us. Going back to our roots is always necessary.

Southern University has taught me so many things about myself and African American culture. I know I could not find or experience what I learned at Southern elsewhere. Every institution has its struggles, but those struggles should never be viewed as such. To us, they are mere circumstances and opportunities for growth, success, and positive change. Louisiana is the cultural heartbeat the United States. Southern University is the mecca of the state. Across the nation, we are known as competitive and a bit bourgeois. We think our institution is the only HBCU. While true, we are also dedicated, gung-ho fans of our athletics and the Human Jukebox. We are proud of our academic programs. Most importantly, we are advocates for our own and for Black culture.

Today, it is still my dream of working in that white building, the Archives building. That gives me hope that one day, our stories will be told and presented with grace and pride. One day, I will have the privilege of serving in a curator capacity to promote the preservation of all of our stories to students and the community.

I stand in purpose, providing the research and life histories of those who should not be forgotten…providing the life histories of those who made the institution what it continues to be:

The Land of the Mighty Jaguars!

About Ja'el Gordon

Ja'el Gordon, Louisiana-born Genealogist and a Historian is a Southern University and A&M College Baton Rouge 2012 graduate with a Bachelor of Arts in History. Always dedicated to her alma mater, Ms. Gordon worked for the Division for Student Affair from 2012 to 2018 where she managed Student Organizations and created a plethora of successful, engaging events and programs for the student body and community. In 2015, Ms. Gordon received her Master of Arts in Museum Studies from Southern University New Orleans and she is currently a Ph.D. Candidate in Jackson State University's Higher Education Ph.D. program. Outside of working in Higher Education, Ms. Gordon has owned her own genealogy business for several years where she provides family history and genetic genealogy research through educational program facilitation.

As an avid researcher, Ms. Gordon specializes in antebellum and enslaved history research in Louisiana and Mississippi. In this capacity she conducts research, provides corrective narratives of the enslaved, and descendant tracing for present and "lost" plantations around the State of Louisiana with special focus on the River Road plantations. She serves as Charter Member and current President of the Louisiana Chapter of Afro American Historical and Genealogical Society and was recently selected as the Historian for Our Genetic Legacy History Maker's Project. She is also a proud member of Delta Sigma Theta Sorority, Inc and Sigma Alpha Iota International Music Fraternity for Women.

Marina Zeno

From Student to Destiny
Marina Zeno

I graduated from Southern University in December 2012 with my BA in Arts and later with my master's degree in business administration in December 2016. The day I received my letter of acceptance from Southern University, I was excited and scared. But I was also elated to be a part of an HBCU, given my history of attending all-white schools throughout my childhood. From the time I was a young girl, I was always taught who I was as an African American from my father, who also graduated from an HBCU. I was filled with such great pride and admiration for my school, and I felt at home the first day on campus. I met a lot of great people in my freshman class of 2008, but I was very precise in getting my work done and being the best student I could be in this new world of knowledge. Even though I was excited to be in college, it was still the hardest semester of my college career. I was not prepared for the workload of seventeen credit hours, being on my own, walking miles to every destination, and keeping up with all the paperwork, books and assignments. I had a lot of anxiety. I wanted to go home, but my friends had study sessions and hangouts at the student union. This made the experience a lot more fun.

During my freshman year, I also had a lot of excited things happen to me. I won two Tyler Perry tickets to "The Marriage Counselor" play at the Southern University Mini Dome. I also attended a Disney College Program seminar where they were recruiting students to complete a semester internship at Walt Disney World in Florida. Since my major was in theatre, I had to jump on the opportunity. The beginning of my sophomore year, I was in Florida, working and taking courses at Walt Disney World. With all of those exciting things, the number one exciting thing that happened to me was when I got to meet my "Shero" Iyanla Vanzant. She had a speaking event at Southern University in the spring of 2008 while promoting one of her books. This was before she made a huge comeback with Oprah or her show, *Iyanla, Fix My Life*. I was so excited, and I was one of the first people at the event. At the time, a lot of my peers did not understand why I was so excited to see just another author or speaker. They didn't understand who she was. There were a lot of people in the ballroom, but it was mostly faculty, grad students and law students. Unbeknownst to her, she became my therapist and counselor since I was a teenager watching her on TV. I never got a chance to talk with her afterward, but that will forever be one of the greatest moments at Southern University for me.

When I came back to school in the spring of my sophomore year, I went back to my normalcy of being a student. But I had lost touch with a lot of my friends, until I entered into the college arts and started taking classes within my major. The Theatre Arts department was smaller than usual, but it made all of the students and professors close to one another, somewhat like family—especially since we were always with each other in class, and for performances, practices and study groups. While I had found a family at Southern, I still had a lot of struggles. Midway through my undergrad career, I had to start paying for my own tuition due to my parent refusing to complete my FASFA. I went to the financial aid office multiple times, but no one was able to help me because of the financial aid laws. They told me that my parent had to complete my FASFA. I could not complete it as an independent student because I was not twenty-four years old yet or in grad school.

So, I started working two jobs while going to school. I moved out of on-campus housing and lived with family members to cut cost. It was the hardest struggle I ever had to face. But with scholarships, deferred tuition payments and even credit cards, I graduated. The day of graduation, I felt so accomplished—not just because I was getting a degree—but because I had so many obstacles that were placed in front of me to quit. But I never did. I just found another way. As I walked across that stage to get my degree, I cried.

When I decided to continue my education through grad school, it was no doubt in my mind that I would go back to my alma mater. I got accepted into the MBA program in the fall of 2014. My first year in the program, I became the vice president of the MBA student association. During my time as a vice president, I, as well as the student association, provided many resources to the College of Business students, such as resume and interviewing skills, as well as free headshots. Being in the Master of Business graduate school, it opened a new world for me professionally. There were a lot of professors who genuinely cared about their students' wellbeing and success. I remember being a part of study sessions that ended sometimes at midnight with our professors, who were helping us make sure that we understood the material and were prepared to pass exams. One professor helped me the most: Dr. Kirk. Dr. Kirk has had a long history of going above and beyond for his students. He was the main marketing professor in the business department. He saw that I took a strong liking to marketing and entrepreneurship. He took me under his wing and also introduced me to a sales organization founded in New Orleans called National Sales Network. During grad school, I became a member and have been a part of the organization for the past six years. National Sales Network has helped me with my professional elevation and enhance my networking skills. I am now the Director of Marketing for the organization. Southern University taught me a lot about myself, including perseverance. My tenure there contributed to a lot of my successes. Today, I am an insurance broker and small business owner.

About Marina Zeno

Marina Zeno is a native of Lafayette Louisiana and a devoted mother to her son Skylar Derouen Jr. She is a SEBD certified small business owner of Marina Zeno Derouen Services LLC where she provides insurance needs for middle class families and individuals as an Insurance Broker. Marina graduated from Southern University at A&M College in 2012 with her Bachelor's degree in Theatre and her Master's in Business Administration in 2016.

During her MBA program she became the Vice President of the Student Association and is currently a prominent member of multiple professional organizations such as National Sales Network Louisiana Chapter where she is the Director of Marketing. Throughout Marina's life she has had immense perseverance and a sheer tenacity for success and growth.

Courtney Cierra Walker

Courtney Walker's HBCU Experience
Courtney Cierra Walker

My HBCU experience at Southern University A&M College was extremely amazing. Both of my parents are proud alumni. My father proposed to my mother on campus. A few years after their marriage, my mother received her degree while she was eight months pregnant with me. I have been a Jaguar fan since birth. As a child, I attended most of the football games. At an early age, I knew I would someday be a proud graduate of Southern University A&M College.

My dream of becoming a student became a reality in the fall of 2010. During the summer of 2010, I received my acceptance letter and attended Jaguar Preview. Once I stepped on the "Yard", I knew I was home. Everything about Southern University is amazing. Now granted, I was never a stranger to the "Yard". My father was a part of the Human Jukebox back in the eighties, so he took my little sister and I to campus often to watch the band practice. Therefore, I was somewhat acclimated with Southern University's layout.

Jaguar Preview thoroughly prepared me for freshman year. During Jaguar Preview, I experienced a glimpse of what it was like to be a student. I temporarily lived on campus and was required to adhere to the schedule provided to me. I was placed in Totty Hall. The roommate I was assigned was remarkably interesting, to say the least. There were several student workers who gave us a tour of the campus. During the tour of our school, I met two amazing people: Kisha and Keady. They became close friends of mine during undergrad. After the tour, I met my advisor, who assisted me with the admissions process and provided me with my school schedule for the fall.

The last night of Jaguar Preview, the Greeks put on a show for us at the meet and greet party. Everyone had so much fun. We were all dancing, singing and getting to know each other until the party ended. The meet and greet party allowed us an opportunity to befriend those who declared the same or similar majors. Before I knew it, the semester started and, thankfully, I was fully prepared to start my journey as a student at the Southern University A&M College.

I remember my first day of freshman year as if it were yesterday. Class started promptly at 8 a.m. I arrived at my English class around 7:45 a.m., prepared to begin my new journey. After introductions, the professor gave us a syllabus and an assignment. The same occurred in all courses thereafter. Once the first day of school was over, I went to Starbucks to grab a Frappuccino, then went home to complete my assignments. I officially became a coffee and Amazon lover during my freshman year of college.

Initially, my major was business management. My parents were entrepreneurs, and I aspired to be like them. My goal was to get my degree in business management, obtain my cosmetology license, and open a beauty salon. Toward the end of the first semester of freshman year, that goal changed. Mr. Turner, my History of Civilization professor, saw potential in me. He always encouraged me to go to law school. He was amazed by my communication and note-taking skills. He constantly used my work as an example of how he expected others to complete their work. Mr. Turner turned me into a professional. I remember showing up to Mr. Turner's class with a bonnet covering my hair. It was raining, and I did not want to mess up my hair. Granted, I shouldn't have entered class with my bonnet on; nonetheless, Mr. Turner politely turned me around at the door. He would not allow me, or anyone else, to enter his classroom wearing a bonnet or anything else unprofessional. From that point on, I never showed up to his class, or anywhere else, in unprofessional (ratchet) attire.

Every Wednesday was considered "Pretty Wednesday" on campus. Every Wednesday, I looked forward to dressing up and attending the highly anticipated fashion show in The Student Union. My friends and I always dressed to impress on Wednesdays. I always wore my fanciest heels and prettiest pearls. As a Southern alumna, I still raise the bar on Wednesdays.

As time progressed, and sophomore year approached, I decided to change my major to political science – prelaw. I must admit that was one of the best decisions I have ever made. As a political science major in an HBCU, I was able to witness issues being addressed by powerful African American leaders in my community, firsthand. I received the opportunity to intern with the Legislative Assistants for Sharon Weston Broome and Tara Wicker. I was also granted an opportunity to intern for the Louisiana Democratic Party. Obtaining experience of such magnitude as a student was life changing.

I realized I was passionate about politics and public policy in 2012, after Trayvon Martin's death. I was in one of Dr. Samuels' politics classes, and he was infuriated with the lack of justice for Trayvon. As African American students, just a little older than Trayvon during that time, we all felt Dr. Samuels' frustration. We all sought justice for Trayvon. The lack of justice for wrongfully murdered African Americans sparked my passion to become an agent for change in my community. My political science professors provided me with the education and resources needed to succeed in politics and the public sector. I received my Bachelor of Arts in Political Science, with honors, in the Fall of 2013.

Not only did Southern University provide me with an excellent education, but it also provided me with nutritious meals. My freshman fifteen was more like freshman twenty-five. The soul food served in the cafeteria was extremely delicious. I surely miss "Fried Fish Fridays" in the cafeteria. The restaurants in the Student Union always served fresh, hot food. I was never disappointed.

Southern University A&M College is the only school I attended that was family-oriented, in every sense of the word. Southern has a Child Development Laboratory on campus, which allows parents to drop off their children prior to attending class. My professors felt like aunts and uncles to me. I had nothing but the utmost respect for them. I always felt as if I was in a family-structured environment. For the most part, each semester, class felt like a family reunion. My classmates and I wanted each other to succeed. We had countless group study sessions, both in person and virtually. To this day, my former classmates and I refer each other for jobs and connect each other to resources, when needed. At Southern, unbreakable bonds are formed.

There is nothing like Southern University's homecoming

festivities. Every day of homecoming week, there is something fun for the students to do. There are comedy shows, fashion shows, concerts with well-known artists, Miss Southern University's Coronation, Greek shows and more. As an undergraduate student, I attended most of Southern University's homecoming festivities and woke up around 7 a.m. on homecoming day to attend the homecoming parade. To this day, homecoming excites me. I enjoy seeing and conversing with other alumni.

Aside from homecoming, the Bayou Classic is another big game day that alumni and students look forward to. During my years as a student, my classmates and I would go shopping together to find the perfect outfits for the Bayou Classic. As soon as thanksgiving dinner ended, we would meet in New Orleans on Bourbon Street and get our "party on". The next day, we would meet at the Superdome for the battle of the bands. Afterward, we partied until the sun came up on game day. On game day, the after-party occurred no matter the outcome of the game.

In the spring of 2016, I attended graduate school. My graduate school experience was not much different from my undergraduate experience. During graduate school, I was a full-time employee; therefore, I was unable to attend all of the festivities that I attended during my undergrad years. I was, however, able to tailgate and attend football games. Of course, as a graduate student, I was held to a higher standard. I was always expected to dress and act professionally. In grad school, I learned how to write grants, analyze policies, manage nonprofit organizations and a plethora of other things. In the spring of 2019, my sister, Melanie Walker, and I graduated together. Melanie was recognized as the top nursing student. She received her Bachelor of Science degree in Nursing, with high honors. I received my Master of Public Administration degree with a concentration in Healthcare Administration.

In conclusion, my overall experience at Southern University A&M College was nothing short of amazing. Southern molded me into the professional I am today. Because of the lessons learned at Southern University, I am a successful business owner.

About Courtney Cierra Walker

Courtney Cierra Walker was born and raised in Baton Rouge, Louisiana. She is a proud Christian who spreads agape love everywhere she goes. At an early age, Courtney discovered her passion for helping others. She has dedicated countless hours to giving back to those who are less fortunate. Courtney has approximately nine years of experience in the public sector. She has managed successful political campaigns in Baton Rouge and New Orleans. She volunteers with several nonprofit organizations and gives back to the community every chance she gets.

Courtney received two degrees from Southern University A&M College. She obtained her undergraduate degree in Political Science, with honors, Fall 2013. Spring 2019, she obtained her Master of Public Administration degree, with a concentration in Healthcare Administration. During graduate school, she learned how to write grants. With the education received in her grant writing course, she began to write grants for others through her freelance writing business, Cici's Freelance Services. Courtney is also the proud owner of an online boutique, Exoticc Soles and Accessories, LLC. Currently, she is employed at a prestigious law firm, Murray & Murray, LLC.

In her spare time, she enjoys spending time with family, cooking, reading books, writing poetry, and conducting research on how to eradicate homelessness in her community. With her education and skillset, she plans to open a nonprofit organization someday. Her goal is to help the less fortunate by providing resources so that they could obtain gainful employment and provide for themselves.

Last but certainly not least, Courtney recently became a mother to a bouncing baby boy, Bryon Linson. He is her prized possession. She is enjoying every second of motherhood. With Bryon as her newfound motivation, she is determined to live life to the fullest and create generational wealth.

Yladrea Drummond, J.D.

Excellence Over Excuses
Yladrea Drummond, J.D.

So, there I stood on the side of the commencement stage, waiting for my moment. They called my name and across the stage I walked. I should've run in case they tried to take the degree back. When people say to me, "Wow! That's awesome that you graduated from law school." I always respond, sometimes out loud and other times in my head, "Barely!" Truth is, I wasn't an A student. I wasn't even a B student. But guess what? I still obtained my Juris Doctorate. And no one can take that from me.

It seems like so long ago, yet it feels like it was yesterday. The experience is one that I will carry for a lifetime. Of course, I didn't just start and magically get my degree overnight. So, let's tap into my journey.

When I entered law school at Southern University Law Center, I was twenty-one years old. No one in my family had ever gone, so I didn't know what to expect. I was so green. The first day of orientation, I pulled up to the door and noticed everyone dressed in a suit. I had on jeans and a t-shirt. Clearly, I'd missed the memo. I hurried back to my apartment and changed into the most professional outfit I could find. I hadn't bought not one suit. Honestly, it never crossed my mind.

But that was only the first glimpse of excellence that I experienced. I soon learned that the expectation of professionalism and excellence was at the core of SULC. I had been around successful Black people, but never had I seen this caliber of Black excellence. Coming from a predominantly White school for undergrad, it was a bit of a culture shock.

Now I grew up engulfed in Black culture, so being among my people was nothing new. However, excellence is a different category. It consumes you. It's what you aspire to obtain. Being at Southern University Law Center provided me with that experience and opportunity.

It all went by so fast. The first year went by, and I noticed that I absolutely hated law school. If this is any representation of what an attorney does in real life, I don't want it. Well at least that's how I originally felt. I later realized that it was because I had never been challenged so much in my life. On top of the rigorous curriculum, learning what professionalism truly looks like was a rough transition. But after surviving the hardest first year of law school, I made it back. For those who don't know, not all who start with you actually finish. In fact, the first year is what I call the chopping block. So, because I made it through, I decided to give it another shot to truly show myself that I can be excellent, too. I realized that telling myself that I disliked SULC, was me being scared to step into greatness and an excuse to be mediocre when times get tough. I'm glad I didn't give up because SULC had so much to teach me and grow me as a woman.

When the second year rolled around, I'd adjusted. I got more competitive in my grades and tried to get more involved. I figured the only way to truly take in the experience was to throw myself into the thick of it. My law school was filled with phenomenally successful attorneys who had thriving careers. They were known for some of the toughest teachers in the state, so I needed to step it up.

The motto of The Law Center was "Seriousness of Purpose." For a while, I was unsure how that fit me. But by the time you finish your journey, it's not about what it means. It's literally how you as an individual will spend the rest of your days walking through life. Let's face it. Your purpose in this world is serious.

I made it through year three and went on to graduate. I was twenty-four years old on the day I graduated. It was one of the highest moments in my life. Look at me, a twenty-four-year-old Black woman with a Juris Doctor, ready to take on the world. That moment only lasted for about a week. I started to realize that I had been moving at full speed through school and had never even had a real adult job. I had no idea of the road ahead or what was next.

All I knew was that The Law Center geared our minds to be strong and to trust that we had the skills to take on whatever was next.

A juris doctor degree is a blessing and a curse. It's a blessing because it displays that you have knowledge of an area that is hard to learn. It's a curse because, if you don't pass the bar exam, you are either overqualified or underqualified. It's never in between. I took the bar three times and didn't pass. So, it sometimes felt like I had been let down. In reality, I just didn't realize the power in having a law degree. I didn't realize how to utilize that power in different areas in the workforce.

So, when I finally figured out how to unleash that power and get the jobs I deserved, I found the much-deserved appreciation for SULC. What I didn't realize was that they taught me how to be direct, persistent and relentless. I learned to never stop at, "No." They taught me to keep applying pressure and to set the standard of excellence, resilience and greatness. In the face of defeat, they showed me there is always a chance to win!

Southern University Law Center is the reason I am fearless. It's the reason that I know how to thrive, even when the odds are stacked against me. It molded me and played a huge role in the woman I've become.

For that, I'll be forever grateful!

About Yladrea Drummond, J.D.

Dr. Yladrea Drummond is a native of Houston, Texas. She is a lawyer, author, black culture advocate, accomplished compliance consultant, political strategist, diversity advisor and leadership trainer. She holds a B.A. in Political Science from Texas State University and a Juris Doctorate from Southern University Law Center. Dr. Yladrea Drummond currently serves as the Special Assistant to the President of the Legal Services Corporation in Washington, D.C., where she assists other great attorneys in expanding equal access to justice.

Dr. Drummond is the Founder of The Ink Up, through which she desires to create a community of affordable literary services and increase exposure to the black literary community, by staying dedicated to strengthening the power of black literature and those behind the pen. Additionally,

she is the Founder & CEO of Capital Strategies, LLC, which is the first black-owned NGO compliance and financial services firm in the United States and ACTIVate a nonprofit with a mission to help the formerly incarcerated make a true transition back into society and thrive. Lastly, Dr. Drummond, alongside other black leaders, became a Cofounder & Senior Legal Advisor of Black Culture Weekly a platform created to revolutionize and centralize media through action for black audiences to have access to the things they believe in and enjoy.

Dr. Drummond believes that limits are meant to hold back a person's inner genius and doesn't see a reason to box herself in. To that end, she released her first self published book, Through These Eyes: Surrendering the Ties of My Soul in September 2020. The book dives deep into how her past trauma played a role in how she moved through life and how breaking her "soul ties" allowed her to become the woman she is today. Dr. Drummond is currently working on her first fiction book and is excited to explore the possibilities of her mind's creativity.

Above all of her accomplishments, Dr. Yladrea Drummond takes pride in her biggest role as a wife and mother of her two sons. She enjoys adventure, cooking new dishes as she pretends to be a contestant on Top Chef, traveling across the world, binge watching TV series and organizing her Happy Planner.

When it's all said and done, Dr. Yladrea Drummond pledges her life's mission, to uplift others, expand access to the underserved, be a vessel for the unheard, and tackle injustice across the nation.

Casey D. Greggs

Southern University: My Only Choice!
Casey D. Greggs

As an African American child in Baton Rouge, Louisiana, more than likely, your parents attended Southern University. Maybe even their parents attended, as well. This made Southern University instantly part of my blood. I bled blue and gold. Even for those students whose parents did not attend Southern, they could feel the culture from miles away. As an African American in Baton Rouge, you couldn't deny the presence and the culture of Southern University.

Both of my parents, and other family members, graduated from Southern University. My grandfather was Dr. Isaac Greggs, the legendary band director of The Human Jukebox. Therefore, I really had absolutely no choice but to bleed blue and gold. At an early age, I saw how special Southern was to my family. Southern University meant family, culture, beauty, fellowship, education and legacy. Almost everyone I grew up with attended Southern University, or they shared in the culture and were impacted by its rich legacy in some way.

As a little girl, my brother, cousins and I spent a lot of our time with the Southern University Marching Band. For me, it was always about the Fabulous Dancing Dolls. They were so beautiful. I wanted to be just like them. My parents always took us to the band room, which later became Dr. Isaac Greggs Band Hall. We went to every game. I loved the band, but I absolutely loved the Dolls. The pretty costumes and glitter shoes always made a bold statement. I always said to myself, "If I wish to become a Dancing Doll, it will come true." So, every birthday, I wished to become a Dancing Doll before blowing out my candles. I was definitely a dreamer. I would even pick dandelions and say, "I want glitter shoes like the Dancing Dolls, and please let me become one when I grow up!" Then, I would blow the seeds away. Well, in the summer of 2009, my wish came true. I became a Fabulous Dancing Doll. I danced for four beautiful years and became a Forever Doll after graduating at the top of my class in 2013.

Southern University taught me so much and contributed so

much to the person I am today. I enrolled into Southern University in hopes of becoming an elementary teacher and a Dancing Doll. While at Southern, I was an elementary education major, Dancing Doll, and a member of the Alpha Tau Chapter of Delta Sigma Theta Sorority, Incorporated. These three major elements made up my experience at Southern. Along with my parents, these things played an equal role in molding me into who I am today.

When you are enrolled into an HBCU, preferably Southern University, your class sizes are smaller. In many cases, the classes will be more intimate. Depending on your major, your professors might even look just like you. This was true for me at Southern. It's unique because when a professor looks just like you, they tend to know how to educate you better. They care about your education and your future, as long as you care about it first. I decided to become an education major to make a difference in children's lives. I wanted to help them make sense of the world and to be a positive influence that can help guide their education. My professors knew my name. I knew I could always look to them for guidance.

My experiences throughout my years in the College of Education taught me how to be professional, how to speak intelligently, how to work well with others, and also how to think critically and problem solve. It might sound a bit cliché, but I promise you it's true. The professors forced us to work in groups many times with classmates who were not our actual friends, but this was a good task to teach us how to work with everyone. They also used real-life examples in every lesson. Specifically, Dr. Kelly, Dr. Kleinpeter, and Dr. Luria Young, whose son I taught years later in second grade, all played a huge role in my success at Southern. Choosing to attend an HBCU, no matter the major, allows you to learn strategies to help you navigate the real world from educators who actually care about you becoming what you learn. They will make you work, but they will make sure it's all worth it in the end.

Now, another plus to attending an HBCU is having the opportunity to join organizations that will absolutely leave long-lasting impacts on your character and life. For me, I chose a Greek organization and became a member of the Alpha Tau Chapter of Delta

Sigma Theta Sorority, Incorporated. When you become a freshman, the first thing you see is all the fun that sororities and fraternities have. They do it all, from step shows and strolling in front of the Student Union, to chants and parties. But, when you truly make a conscious effort to join, you see that these elements are not what makes sororities and fraternities so great. It's the programs they provide for students, including bringing in experienced panelists to teach about real life, the community service that they are involved in, and the sisterhood and brotherhood they cultivate. Becoming a Delta meant that I would gain lifelong friendships and sisterhood, and that I would have direct pathways to community service that would help me make a difference. Being in a sorority teaches you history, respect, sisterhood, how to be a lady, and even how to own a room with pride and dignity. When you join a Greek organization, you are committed for life. You learn many lessons and reap benefits that help mold you into a beautiful person.

Before I expound on how amazing it was to be a Southern University Dancing Doll, and how it truly impacted the woman I am today, please let me emphasize how important it is to become a member of any organization at your university. Becoming a part of an organization allows you to explore the world, gain friendships, and learn so much. Organizations allow you to fail and make mistakes, but they will teach you how to keep your head up and finish strong. Most importantly, organizations will teach you how to communicate, love, co-exist and become a well-rounded individual. Most lessons are usually in disguise, but they are always present.

Being a Southern University Dancing Doll taught me patience, love, respect, kindness, compassion, how to carry myself like a lady, how to co-exist, how to delete excuses from my vocabulary, and definitely how to problem solve. It gave me sisters and friendship, and it has given me legacy and lifelong connections to Southern University. We had so many opportunities as young adults to not only perform for our beautiful fans and cheer on the football team, but to travel and grace big stages beyond A.W. Mumford Stadium. We were honored to perform for Super Bowls and with big recording artists.

HBCUs prepare you for your future. They give you the necessary tools to succeed. You will find yourself walking into the purpose that God has intended for you. When you graduate and begin your next chapter, and you're met with conflict, think about how you were taught to find a resolution for conflict in your organization. When you run into a difficult co-worker, or even boss, think about how you were taught to be professional and respectful, but to be firm and always stand up for yourself. Lastly, remember to always think about how you learned to love and what it takes to sustain genuine friendships.

You will gain everything you need to navigate life mentally. Attending an HBCU is what gives you those special tools to hold onto, no matter where you decide to go in life. I used my tools from Southern to become a highly qualified teacher, which led me into earning my master's degree in Educational Leadership, and I am now a school counselor. I will always hold on to every experience from Southern. I'm certain that I wouldn't be where I am today without Southern University and A&M College in Baton Rouge, Louisiana.

Forever a Jaguar.

Forever a Delta. Forever a Southern University Dancing Doll!

About Casey D. Greggs

Casey Danielle Greggs was born in Baton Rouge, Louisiana, raised in Zachary, Louisiana, and is 29 years old. She completed elementary school at Zachary Elementary and was a member of the Beta Club while in elementary school. She completed middle and high school at Southern University Laboratory School in Baton Rouge.

While at Southern Lab, Casey was a member of the basketball team, track team, volleyball team, softball team, cheerleading team, and was a Dancing Doll. She was also a member of the mock trial team and the Southern University Laboratory band in middle school where she played the clarinet.

While in high school, she also participated in organizations outside of her school and was a member of Louisiana Leadership Institute in Baton Rouge, where she was a Dazzling Starlette Dancer. She was also a member of Lambda Tau youth sorority.

After receiving her diploma in 2009 from Southern Lab, graduating with Magna Cum Laude honors, she went on to attend her family's legacy university, Southern University and A&M College in Baton Rouge, LA. While at Southern University, Casey was a 4-year Dancing Doll and was a member of the Alpha Tau Chapter of Delta Sigma Theta Incorporated.

Casey was on the Dean's list from 2009-2013, graduated as the top student in the College of Education, and was the Student Marshall for the graduating class of 2013. She went on to become a 2nd grade teacher in Zachary, Louisiana where she taught for 6 years, and later went on to receive her master's degree in Education Leadership from Louisiana State University Shreveport.

She is currently teaching 2nd grade but made the leap into the virtual world 2 years ago and absolutely loves it. Casey has hopes of soon becoming an assistant principal at her current job and she owes it all to her first love, her HBCU, Southern University!

Christal Williams

Living Her Dreams
Christal Williams

After graduating from Washington Marion Magnet High School, I embarked on a journey to attend Southern University, not knowing that would be my home for the next four years of my life. I had so many doubts about being away from home. I thought to myself, *Am I really going away to college?* I always wanted to be a registered nurse, but I never knew what school I wanted to go to. Upon entering high school, I researched HBCUs. I gravitated toward Southern University since my junior year in high school due to their highly reputable nursing program. After applying to many other universities, and getting accepted and visiting colleges, my final decision came down to Southern University.

I had visited the campus of Southern University during a high school tour. My family moved me onto campus in August of 2001. I experienced mixed feelings when move-in day arrived. I felt fear, excitement and doubt about going away to school and being away from my family. But little did I know, this was only the beginning of my journey at Southern University that changed my life. When my family left, I wondered how I was going to do things on my own. *Am I setting myself up for failure by going away to school?* On a positive note, my roommate was my best friend of many years from my hometown. I developed connections with new friends, as well as peers from my hometown, where we encouraged each other to do well in school. The culture on campus was what helped me make a smooth college transition. Everyone on campus was like one big family.

I was introduced to some unique things on campus that only a Southern University graduate could relate to, such as fried chicken Mondays at Dunn Hall, Pretty Wednesdays at the Union, and the famous Blue Store. Although there were so many social activities on campus, I found myself in my dorm room studying most of the time. The university also promoted high scholastic achievement through university forums on various topics of concern for college students.

I immediately felt comfortable with my college transition,

despite missing my family. I received so much more than my bachelor's degree in nursing at Southern University. Southern University instilled so many characteristics in me that helped mold me into the person I am today. I sometimes look at my life and realize that a lot of my life decisions were influenced through the wisdom I gained at SU. My motto was, "Failure is not an option." Southern University challenged me, but I turned those challenges into the successes that I have accomplished today.

Thanks to my mentors, which were my professors, I learned the value of hard work and to never give up, no matter what obstacles were faced during my academic journey. My nursing department had many great professors with so much wisdom. I looked up to these individuals as role models. I met faculty and advisors who encouraged me. They wanted to see me grow and succeed. My former professors' commitment and passion inspired me to follow in their path and obtain my master's in Nursing Education and pursue a career in academia.

I had great support from many of my old peers from my hometown, as well as new peers. I gained friends from different walks of life and I experienced different aspects of African American culture. After I was accepted into the clinical component of nursing school, I was introduced to an awesome new group of friends who shared the same major. We studied together, prayed together, and pushed each other to do our absolute best in school. It was encouraging to be around peers who share common goals and expectations. They wanted success just as bad as I wanted it.

My junior year of college, I became a member of the Beta Psi Chapter of Alpha Kappa Alpha Sorority, Incorporated. This was an experience I will never forget. My sorority positively impacted and shaped my life. I was aware of a few Greek organizations, but I never knew what the Divine Nine organizations were until my enrollment at Southern University. Joining this sorority brought many opportunities for me while in college, such as lifelong friendships and an opportunity to participate in community service activities. I was able to meet prestigious individuals who made an impact on and off campus and in the Baton Rouge community.

I was the vice president of my senior nursing class, which helped me develop leadership and teamwork skills.

When my graduation day arrived, I felt accomplished. I looked back on my years at Southern University and realized how I was initially homesick and scared. I always missed my family. I am forever grateful for the many sacrifices my parents made for me to be able to attend college. I am thankful that I took advantage of my opportunities at Southern University, which influenced my growth as a person. I always say, "I lived my college years." I would not be the person I am today without the valuable experiences at Southern University.

My priority for enrolling in college was academics. However, I am so grateful for my HBCU experience. The culture and history of attending an HBCU is unexplainable. Southern University has molded me into the woman I am today. The friendships and lessons experienced enriched my life. I knew that, even if I failed, I would pick up the pieces and try again while in college. College challenged me and provided me with the necessary tools to be successful. After graduating, I realized I could accomplish anything, which pushed me to continue my education and become an aspiring entrepreneur. I never would have thought I would value the education I received at Southern University the way I do today. When I speak on Southern University, it is always with great pride and joy! I am a proud, first-generation Southern University HBCU graduate!

I now reside in Lake Charles, Louisiana and have been married for eleven years to my wonderful husband Anthony. I have two handsome sons, AJ and Aiden, and a stepdaughter, Nadia. I always stress the importance of education to my children.

About Christal Williams

Christal Williams was born and raised in Lake Charles, LA. She is a 2006 graduate of Southern University Baton Rouge. She graduated with a Bachelor of Science in Nursing Degree. She continued her education and is a 2013 graduate from Lamar University where she earned a Master's Degree in Nursing with a concentration in Nursing Education.

Christal was initiated in the Beta Psi Chapter of Alpha Kappa Alpha Sorority, Incorporated in Fall 2003 on the campus of Southern University and she is still an active member in the Zeta Psi Omega chapter in Lake Charles, LA. She is a member of the Southern University Alumni Chapter as well as the Southern University Alumni Lake Charles Chapter. Christal serves as a member of many professional organizations and currently serves as a board member for the Lake Charles District Nurses Association. She is also on the membership committee for the Louisiana State Nurses Association.

Today, Christal resides in Lake Charles, LA where she is an Assistant Professor in the College of Nursing and Health Professions at McNeese State University. She has been married to her amazing husband Anthony for 11 years and she has a step-daughter and 2 sons. She is also an entrepreneur where her and her husband owns First Choice Medical Transportation Services, LLC and First Choice Personal Care Services, LLC.

Brittany M. Lee

Forever, I love Southern U.
Brittany M. Lee

Historically Black Colleges and Universities (HBCUs) have provided the means for African Americans to excel through education when others wouldn't allow us through their doors. The experience is invaluable. You will find friends, family and yourself. The memories will last a lifetime.

The Decision (2001 – 2005)

I distinctly remember the day I decided I was going to be a Southern Jaguar. I was in the eighth grade. I attended a "Black College" recruiting fair at Valley High School in Sacramento, California. My aunt was with me, and I was amazed. This was the first time I recall being exposed to HBCUs. The auditorium was full. Students, parents and school representatives were everywhere, and the energy was captivating. I must have circled the room three or four times before I worked up enough nerve to visit a booth. For some reason, I believed the recruiters would see that this was my first event, and I was anxious. After getting my nerves under control, I listened to the recruiters at each booth. I was fascinated, intrigued and engaged. Once I made it to the Southern University booth, Dr. Robert Rene, who was recruiting on the West Coast at the time, greeted everyone and excused the parents. He only wanted to speak with the students. Dr. Rene asked how many of us had taken the PSAT or ACT prep course. I hadn't at the time. What set his recruitment appeal apart from any of the others I heard that day was that he wanted us to be prepared even as junior high school students. It *felt* right. Southern was on my mind from that day forward.

While my other counterparts in high school were wondering what colleges they would apply to, I had already chosen Southern. I was a decent student, and I was confident I would be accepted. During my senior year of high school, the "Black College" recruiting fair made its way to my high school, Natomas High School. To my surprise, Dr. Rene was back as the recruiter. This time, I was a bit more ready. It had to be SU. Southern University and A&M

College was the only option for me. I applied to other schools, and I was accepted into a number of great HBCUs. But the "Southern U Experience" had already motivated me to become a Jaguar.

The same year, my mother's unit was activated for Operation Iraqi Freedom. She would be leaving for training and deployment, and she would miss my high school graduation. She also wouldn't be able to move me to Southern University. It was tough for all of us. I considered staying in Sacramento just to be near family. My grandmother "Grams" advised me that I should continue with my plans, and I did.

The Experience (2005 -2011)

My first time on "The Yard" was at Jaguar Preview in the summer of 2005. My aunt and my cousin, who was also interested in Southern, were with me. The humidity when you first step off the plane takes some getting used to. I looked at this experience as an adventure. I was jumping into the deep end of transitioning from high school to college. Not only had I decided on a university roughly two thousand miles from my family, but I was moving to a new state I'd never visited before. Thankfully, my mother has first cousins close who became surrogate parents. Their sons, my cousins, became my brothers.

Moving into Alice Boley Hall was an experience. I hadn't shared a room with anyone other than my older sister. I rarely slept over at friends' houses during my childhood. Now I would have a roommate and seven suitemates. Dorm life wasn't at all what I expected. Somehow, it was even better. It wasn't without its issues, but we worked through them. I met some of my best friends my freshman year During the fall of 2005, Hurricane Katrina devastated New Orleans and part of Baton Rouge. Southern University at Baton Rouge became a shelter and home campus for displaced students. Our dorms, campus and classrooms were packed to capacity. It was an unfortunate circumstance that brought about some of the most amazing times.

Academically, I needed a challenge. So, I joined the College of Business and became a marketing major, concentrating in professional sales. To know me is to know that, at the time, I wasn't a "people person." I was introverted and quiet. My major changed me and forced me to grow outside of my comfort zone. It caused me to push past my insecurities. I sharpened my presentation etiquette and developed my public speaking persona. We learned how to interview properly and dress professionally. We were prepared for the industry. I graduated with my Bachelor of Science in Marketing with a concentration in Professional Sales in the spring of 2009. My family from California and Alabama cheered me on as I crossed the stage.

The College of Business became my second home during my matriculation as a student in the Master of Business Administration program. The program was rigorous; yet, the faculty and staff were always available to help. The Dean of the College of Business, who taught my Economics course, came in on weekends to help us understand and apply the material.

During my graduate matriculation, I worked as a graduate assistant for Dr. Joyce O'Rourke during her time as Department Chair of the College of Arts and Humanities. I also worked as a rush cashier, then interim general merchandiser of the Southern University Bookstore for then manager John Dyar. Working two part-time jobs, while pursuing my graduate degree, was difficult. But it taught me to balance my studies and my work. I was also able to learn valuable tools I used later in my career. My mentor, who had been pushing me since my bachelor's degree, helped push me through my graduate program. Through her, I gained "CoB siblings." I graduated with my Master of Business Administration in the spring of 2011.

The Bond (2011 – Present)

Southern University prepared me for life. The struggles, the difficulties and the obstacles I experienced while on "The Yard" made me a more well-rounded person and professional. I entered the corporate world with the knowledge, skills and ability to command my field and excel in my work environment. Southern University has never been far from my mind or heart. The confidence I gained during my time on campus fueled my passion for industry. I wanted to make a difference. I wanted to make a change.

Professionally, I have had the opportunity to work in small local businesses and for larger corporations. After graduating with my master's degree, I joined Walmart Stores as a Manager in Training for Sam's Club #6527 Siegen Lane in August of 2011. Everything I learned in my undergraduate, graduate program and work experiences on campus, I was able to put into practice. After leaving Sam's Club, I worked for a local I.T. company, Dot Calm. Then, I worked as an instructional designer at Louisiana State University. I've also been consulting with businesses for the past five years and I've had the pleasure of seeing them impacted. I also sit on the Business Department Advisory Board for Baton Rouge Community College.

Currently, I am an instructor and advisor in my beloved College of Business. Since joining "The CoB" as a faculty member, I have been passionate about seeing students become the best versions of themselves. It has been my privilege and honor to mentor twelve students from college to career. It is my hope that "The Brittees" know what an inspiration they have been to my life. When I was asked to come back as a part of the faculty to teach, I was honestly apprehensive. I didn't think I had much to contribute to the students. I hadn't been away from school, and I wasn't sure I would be well received. My former professors are now my colleagues. I am ever grateful for my Southern University experience. There's no place else I would have rather received my education and developed myself. I have recruited students, spoken on panel discussions, presented research at conferences and excelled in my life.

But life wouldn't be the same if it wasn't for Southern.

About Brittany M. Lee

A native Californian by way of Sacramento, Brittany is a Spring 2009 and Spring 2011 Graduate of The Esteemed Southern University and A&M College at Baton Rouge, College of Business – A Proud Defender of the Gold and Blue. She earned her Bachelor's in Marketing and Professional Sales and a Master of Business Administration during her matriculation. Brittany has also earned various certifications including one in Hospitality and Tourism Management from Florida Atlantic University. Over the last 10+ years she has held positions as the General Merchandiser for the Southern University Bookstore, Grocery Produce Manger (Merchandiser) – Sam's Club Denham Springs, Instructional Designer at Louisiana State University and is currently an Instructor and Advisor in her beloved College of Business. She has also consulted for the last six years with small businesses in the Baton Rouge area.

Brittany is a proud member of Delta Sigma Theta Sorority Incorporated - Baton Rouge Sigma Chapter, Grand Chaplain of Nia Grand Chapter, Order of the Eastern Star, and member of the Advisory Board – Business Department Baton Rouge Community College. She serves as a Mentor to 12 "Britees" and is the Advisor to the Marketing and Sales Club.

Whenever a free moment occurs, Brittany enjoys volunteering in the Community with her Service Organizations, Mentoring, reading and avoiding learning the acoustic guitar. Brittany's favorite roles are that of daughter, sister, God-Mother, Aunt, niece, friend and cousin. She attends Bethany Church where she has worshipped since moving to Baton Rouge in 2005.

Reuben Lael

Becoming Freshman Class President
Reuben Lael

The best way to describe my first day on campus was a culture shock. I was definitely a fish out of water. Getting out of Dallas ultimately was the goal. Check. Despite my many insecurities of being an only child, and not always the most popular kid in high school, being away from home was new territory. I didn't know much about Louisiana or the culture, but this was my do-over. It was a fresh start on my terms.

Thoughts were scattered as I stood in line at Jones Hall, wondering if my roommate would be cool or the roommate from hell. I watched every episode of *College Hill* and the dorm rooms I saw on TV were for upperclassmen, not freshmen.

"Welcome to the circle," they said.

One thing was for sure: That suite bathroom was clean. Spotless, I tell you. All eight mothers took their own individual turns cleaning the bathroom. How well it was maintained months later was scary. Let's just say ... I did my time.

Of course, my parents were thrilled about my decision to attend a historically black college and university. I have my Spanish teacher from high school to thank. I'm super grateful she made me apply, which wasn't hard after she took me to The Bayou Classic.

I was one of the fortunate ones who didn't have to stand in a long financial aid line. So, all that was left for me to do was to attend freshman orientation. It was a nonstop party from sundown to sunup, and I was having the time of my life.

Each day we were introduced to different campus departments, student organizations and administrators. The union was packed every day during lunch with a DJ, vendors and campus organizations information tables.

In the midst of all the *"jiggalating"* and *"New Orleans shuffles"*, there were a lot of options. But the one that caught my eye was SGA, the Student Government Association.

As a political science major, being a student leader was only natural. Believe it or not, before there was Barack Obama, I dreamed of being the first Black President of the United States of America. In 1998, my mom was elected as the first African-American school board member in my hometown. Watching her fight for justice was something I was immensely proud of and aspired to do. Running for freshman class president was the start of that journey.

I quickly learned that student government at Southern University was no joke. In order to run, every candidate was required to take a comprehensive test overview of the student government constitution. "Don't fail..." they said as they shared horror stories where students failed by one question. There was no retake. Fortunately for me, I passed my constitution test with flying colors, which made me eligible to begin my campaign the following week. There was much excitement on campus about the incoming freshman class. Little did I know, the state of Louisiana had a preferred candidate for freshman class president ... and it was not me.

Politics and public service was the family business. I definitely utilized my parents' resources to create campaign yard signs, which were delivered in person days before my campaign. Between me and my dad, we flooded the campus with my signs. You would have thought I was running for a local seat. Bright and early Monday morning, I was dressed to impress from head to toe with my button-down shirt, tie, slacks and dress shoes. I was determined to show my classmates I was the man for the job.

Walmart owes me a sponsorship deal. Those rollback prices saw me every night to purchase supplies for my campaign. The school shuttle bus ran at 9 P.M. every night for free. My graphic design skills were nowhere close to what they are now. But between me and my printer, I still had the magic sauce. Instead of buttons, I use mailing labels as stickers. Of course, when asking people to vote for you, they will say anything to get free candy and snacks. So, I really couldn't tell if I had a chance, but I wasn't here to lose. I didn't miss a beat. I was a student worker in the political science department, which got me a lot of support and free copies for my campaign signs to hang around campus, which went missing every day. You could say this was one of the benefits of working on campus.

The biggest event during the campaign was the Miss Freshman pageant. It was a sold-out event from wall to wall. The student body marveled at all the contestants in more ways than one, especially during the swimsuit scene. It was clear a lot of these young ladies had been dreaming about this day since birth, with hopes of one day running for Miss Southern.

A few upperclassmen advised me to create an alliance with one of the Miss Freshman contestants. It was a great idea, but not the easiest to execute. Most of the contestants were Louisiana natives and high school friends with my opponent, or a friend of a friend. This made me nervous because we were in a popularity contest. I've always had a heart for the people and took the job representing them seriously. But now I was unsure if I had a chance to win.

The week flew by. After the pageant, all the attention went to the upcoming football game, which happened to be in Houston. Student government was sponsoring a spirit bus to travel to the game. Seats were limited and going fast. I wrestled with if I would pay my deposit, but I decided not to go to the game, given I had just got away from Texas. There was no point in going back.

I was shocked by how quickly the yard became a ghost town. Everybody went to the football game in Houston, including my opponent. The election wasn't until Monday, so most campaigning had stopped. Plus, I was out of candy.

Not really in the mood to even think about the campaign, a quick conversation with my roommate at the time changed that quickly. He was an out-of-state student, as well. Next thing I knew, I was back on the shuttle to Walmart with my last $20. I bought some styrofoam cups and two big bags of popcorn to persuade more voters before election day.

I wasn't into the club scene just yet. There was enough to get into on campus. This time, I switched it up. I put on some jeans and a nice polo instead and stood outside the girls' dormitory, handing out cups of popcorn all Saturday evening. With my opponent missing in action, it quickly made me the man on campus.

By Sunday morning at breakfast in Dunn Hall, I was the people's candidate. As the spirit bus returned to campus later that evening, I restocked on two more bags of popcorn after asking my dad for some extra cash.

Election day was nerve-racking. The popcorn blitz over the weekend had yielded much success and definitely upset the competition and their supporters. The hate was real. I dare not repeat what they said, but it was obvious that I made them mad. At 5 P.M., the polls closed. In less than an hour, I found out I was the 2004-2005 freshman class president.

For me, this was a huge accomplishment as an out-of-state student. As president, I became a member of the royal court, which came with a free wardrobe, travel and lodging to all of the football games, including The Bayou Classic. I was official and had VIP status on the yard. It was a good year!

Before completing my term, I faced many more challenges. I learned a lot about myself and how to serve others. It wasn't easy. The naysayers never went away, but I never let their negativity distract me from my goals. I cherish this experience because it was the beginning of my HBCU journey that I wouldn't trade for anything in the world.

About Reuben Lael

Reuben Lael is a local artist, activist, and organizer. Across DFW, his creative and one-of-a-kind talent is one of Dallas' best-hidden secrets. A proud native of Dallas, Reuben is the son of the Rev. Dr. Roosevelt A. Griffin and Trustee Linda L. Reed-Griffin. His love for servant leadership and music started in the church founded by his parents, St. Mark Baptist Church in Garland, Texas. His love for music started in the church as a singer in the youth choir and a musician for the male chorus and later the entire music department at 16 years old. Reuben was active in school groups including the marching band, a capella choir and was a founding member of the step team in 2002. This group advocates for black student groups and a year black history program. In his senior Reuben advanced to the TMEA all state choir and received a performing arts IB endorsement at graduation.

He is A proud graduate of Southern University and A&M College with a bachelor's and master's in political science and public administration. While at Southern, Reuben was highly involved instead of organizations. His journey began his freshman class president in 2004 and various with a student government association including administrative assistant to the president. In 2006, He served as president of the collegiate 100 black man of metropolitan Baton Rouge. Reuben was also a member of the University concert choir and gospel choir where is joined the beta zeta chapter of mu phi epsilon international music fraternity, inc. In the Spring of 2007 to the Beta Sigma chapter of alpha phi alpha at Southern University.

Reuben became well know for Helping students As an orientation leader every summer during his undergraduate years. As a graduate student, he began his professional career with various departments including Admissions, graduate school, and the Ombudsman office. Now back in Texas, Reuben has 10+ years of career experience as a university administrator for various colleges including the Dallas County Community College District and the University of Texas at Dallas. Since college, he has been faithfully active in Alpha Phi Alpha Fraternity, Inc. and has served in various leadership capacities with the state and southwestern region. Currently, Reuben is an chapter advisor to the Iota Kappa chapter at Paul Quinn College as well as the parliamentarian for the Alpha Sigma Lambda alumni chapter. For his service and community impact, he was honored in 2020 as the Brother of the Year.

Like his father, Reuben is an entrepreneur. In 2017, he launched his brand and media design company *Reuben Lael Media* that aims to creatively support business owners and small businesses by providing high-quality media content. This includes all types of graphic design, music production, and film. In 2019, he answered the call to return to education as a fine arts instructor in Oakcliff at O.W. Holmes Middle School to continue to open pathways to success for black students.

He currently serves on the national board for the National Urban League Young Professionals where he leads the communications team in branding their initiatives to support the national advocacy campaigns, voter engagement, and community outreach since august 2019. He's been a member of DFWULYP since 2015 and is a former executive board member and 2016 member of the year. Reuben was selected as a 2018-2019 National Urban League Emerging Leader.

Among all of his involvements, he is also known for his amazing talent as a singer/songwriter and live entertainer. His thrilling performances bring a message of love, joy, and living your best life! Since his start as a lead vocalist for an open mic band in college, Reuben has performed on many stages across the country including, The Dallas Symphony Myerson, Good Morning Texas and The Black Academy of Arts and Letters to name a few. He also works with many youth fine arts enrichment programs in the city and leads the Garland NAACP fine arts in the community initiative with Garland isd and the city of Garland that provide a free workshop to youth as part of a choir celebration for MLK holiday in Garland. His latest single "Stand Up" is available on all digital platforms and is receiving great reviews for its empowering lyrics inspired by movement and the ongoing fight for justice for Black people and communities in America.

During pandemic, Reuben has used his platforms and artistry

to help bring a new awareness to advocacy and voting to Millenials. Following in the steps of his mother who has served on the Garland ISD School Board since 1998, he organized a local initiative to increase voter turnout in black communities across Dallas. In summer 2020 he with colleagues from "Our Vote Is Our Vote" coalition in Dallas organized "Pack the Polls" car caravan that received high media attention. Over 100 cars participated in the caravan that traveled through communities in Pleasant Grove, South Dallas, and Oakcliff to encourage residents to vote and early vote in both the July primary and presidential election. The event was sponsored by the NAACP, DFW Urban League, Dallas NPHC, and many other local social justice and community organizations.

Monique Walker-Johnson

The Southern University Experience
Monique Walker-Johnson

Picture this: You hail from Atlanta, affectionately called "The Black Mecca" by many. Yet, in an effort to keep you in schools with the greatest number of resources, your parents park you at a predominantly white school for your primary and secondary years. Yes, that's me, Monique Walker-Johnson. One of the only Black faces in my advanced courses. This alone charts my experience at The Southern University. Can you imagine the amazement I experienced when I sat in classes with the majority of scholars who looked just like me? Articulating and answering questions in a way that many times had me suspended in allure because it was what I could only wish for in my educational upbringing. The culture shock was too real and much needed to shape the human being I would continue becoming. Ultimately, I learned so much more about my self due to relation and proximity of my people.

My time at Southern University was much more than about obtaining a degree. It was both literally and figuratively about joining and continuing a legacy of Black excellence. Attending SU reminded me of my capabilities and how Black people have paved the way for scholarship, creative arts, activism and progress in this country. For instance, when I took African American literature, my professor opened my mind to all possibilities just from exposing my roots. Learning about traditions and customs that we see and do every day, and the history of how and why they began, allowed me to see the importance of my heritage. It also allowed me to see how important my culture is as it relates to the makeup of America.

Besides my colleagues, my most memorable experiences were from my professors. My professors had all been where I wanted to go. They had the tools and strategies to equip and prepare me to get where I needed and deserved to be in life. They displayed an unconditional love of pouring important lessons and skills into me. Many of these skills and lessons, I implement daily. The professors in all my programs of study made their mark in their respective fields. They showed my generation of students how to do the same.

The challenges they set forth instilled the hard work, dedication and determination to achieve success through all my adversaries.

By attending Southern, I was essentially charged with not only educating myself, but educating others. I am a mentor and aspiring instructor in my field. I take my activism and sense of justice and equality I learned at Southern, and I use it to create educational opportunities for my mentees and students in Atlanta. I strive daily to encourage Black youth to be the next generation of greatness. It's so important for me to pour into this next generation and generations to come. We have to keep our storyline of experiences going. From my first day of standing in the financial aid line to the last day when I walked across the stage, and every moment in between, I was motivated to elevate my mindset. I had a strong understanding of the role I would play in society. I knew I wanted to be an entrepreneur. I knew I wanted to be a force in my community.

I could not talk about my experiences at Southern without mentioning my opportunity to cross the burning sands and become a member of the Alpha Tau Chapter of Delta Sigma Theta, Incorporated. When I first encountered the women of Alpha Tau, I was intrigued. I knew I wanted to be a part of this organization prior to attending Southern University. But once I saw the magnitude and movement of the Alpha Tau Chapter, I knew that's where I needed to be. One of the greatest things about pledging for me was that I learned the true meaning of humility, which has taken me far in life. I had to push my mind, body and soul to limits that seemed impossible. I developed a mental toughness and resolve that I didn't know I had. I told myself to stay on course. Because of this discipline, my grades were at the highest. Once I crossed the burning sands, it did become more challenging. As a Delta at Southern, I learned how to run a company after running my chapter. From bookkeeping, planning events, running day-to-day business, setting goals, meeting deadlines and even negotiating contracts, I was prepared. I got a full dose of what it takes to make something out of nothing. That is most definitely an experience that made me the businesswoman I am today.

I proudly display my Southern paraphernalia, just waiting on someone to ask about my experience. It makes me so proud to be a part of the Jaguar Nation. It even feels amazing to see my fellow alumni in uniform with me. We are the elite society of Black excellence. The Southern University alumni are resilient and resourceful. Attending Southern cultivated my confidence both personally and professionally. The greatest thing is to be able to call on fellow alumni for opportunities. More importantly, it's to be able to do the same for them. It's about building the community and making our community greater. This is what I learned stepping on campus for the first time as a young, insecure young woman. This transformed me into the courageously resilient woman I am today.

Graduation day was such a pivotal moment in my tenure at Southern University. I will never forget it. I had so many mixed emotions. My colleagues and I were so anxious to finally become alumni. But more importantly, we knew our student life had come to an end. We gained lifetime friends, sisterhoods, brotherhoods and so much more. These connections are forever tokens in my life. It's so good to look back and see how far we have made it from being on the yard at Southern. It's a true honor to bleed blue and gold. It's even more of an honor to be a part of the alumni nation with collective experiences and charges to continue to make the Jaguar Nation great.

About Monique Walker- Johnson

Monique W. Johnson a Southern University Alum and Native of Atlanta,Georgia is an experienced makeup artist of 16yrs. She has had the amazing opportunity to Manage MAC stores in Atlanta for 5yrs. After her tenure at MAC she worked as a freelance makeup artist and moved to New Orleans, LA to work in Film. She has worked on many feature films and TV shows such as: Video Girl, Green Lantern, Twilight, 21 Jump Street, Pitch Perfect, American Horror Story, DJango Unchained, Underground and more. After having her first child she decided to peruse her passion which is working one on one with women in beautification.

She obtained her esthetics license and while in school Monique created her own natural skincare line, Sugar Honey Iced Tea Skincare. Monique recently moved back home to Atlanta to Persue bigger opportunities in the beauty industry.

Shala Washington

Southern Made
Shala Washington

Bayou Classic 2007 is what started my HBCU experience at *the* Southern University A&M. It was my senior year. I had narrowed down my final two college choices to Southern University A&M in Baton Rouge, Louisiana, or Hampton University in Hampton, Virginia. Both were HBCUs. I did not apply to a college that was not an HBCU. I grew up watching *A Different World* and *School Daze,* and I was totally intrigued with the idea of attending a historically black college or university. The history behind both universities is impeccable and very much a part of the culture. When it came time to decide, I was really focused on Hampton. My maiden name was Hampton. The history and legacy of the school was one that I was familiar with. My mom told me to visit some other options, and I did. My mom decided that we attend an event that included the schools. My mom found one event pertaining to Southern University, while I was invited to an event by Hampton University's alumni in Austin, Texas. The invitation came by mail shortly after my acceptance to Hampton University.

Hampton's alumni event came up first. I was living in Killeen, Texas at the time, and Austin was only about an hour away. That hour drive felt like four hours. I was so nervous, which is unlike me. I have always been an outgoing, talkative and sociable person. So, the anxiousness had me feeling like that. I was nervous because college was the first big deal, and first real decision, I'd made by myself as a young adult. We got to the event, and it was an awkward feeling at first. I was one of the few prospective students who did not know anyone at the event. Others either went to the same high school, or their parents were classmates. We had light refreshments and we did an icebreaker. Then, the presentation began. During the presentation, it all became too much for me. The rules, the dress code, the curfew, the limitations on freshmen and out-of-state students. My dad was active-duty military, and that is not what I wanted to sign up for at the time. Now granted, there are going to be rules everywhere. But I wanted to still have some type of freedom and fun while experiencing college.

The event my mom chose for us to attend was The Bayou Classic in New Orleans. I had never been to New Orleans or even heard of The Bayou Classic! I had a few friends in Killeen who were attending Grambling and mentioned us going to them. My coworker played soccer and was a student at Grambling. She basically described The Bayou Classic as a must-attend event. I got excited because I wanted to see what all the hype was about! We left the day after Thanksgiving and stayed at The Sheraton on Canal. So, we were not far from the excitement in the French Quarter. The whole way to New Orleans from Killeen, by the time we got closer to the Louisiana/Texas border, all I saw were Grambling and Southern flags on the cars we passed. I figured they all had to be going to New Orleans, too, for the Classic! Me and my younger siblings counted the number of flags from each school. This was the era where internet and data were not accessible like it is today. I am from the era where you must make do with what you have.

Once we got to New Orleans, I fell in love with the atmosphere – the people, the food, the music, the noise. It was so vibrant, bright and welcoming. Almost everyone we walked past spoke and they were hospitable. On the day of the game, I was sold on the idea of going to Southern University for college. They won the game, the halftime show was amazing, and the band put on an awesome performance. I was in awe of the whole experience. Before I left New Orleans, I knew that Southern was for me! After the Bayou Classic, I was so ready to go to college! Before the fall semester, I attended a Jaguar Preview session in the summer. There was a tour, talks, presentations and rules – but the environment was different from what I had experienced with Hampton's event. Some of the people I attended the Jaguar Preview with became my classmates and friends.

My parents supported whatever decision I made. They were just elated that I decided to go to college. Being a product of teenage parents, where my mom was only fourteen years old when she gave birth to me, I was ready to bring a change to my family. I come from a family of strong women, maternal and paternal. Their strength was instilled in me when I was born. I just did not realize my actual strength until later in my adulthood. Breaking generational curses and doing things differently was a goal of mine. At Southern, there were many students who were like me, while there were some who were not. Some students were parents of alumni. Some students' parents did not attend college at all. Some did not have a relationship with their parents. But coming to Southern made everyone connected. We were family.

When I stepped on the yard in the fall of 2008, I had bright hair and a grill, and I wore tennis shoes almost every day to class. My style and appearance did not bother my professors or my classmates. It didn't deter me from getting the education I did. The professors that became my mentors in undergrad are still my mentors, with many of them being my colleagues now. After graduation, I returned to Southern for grad school, continuing my education with many of my same professors. After my graduation, I soon became a part of The Southern University System. The same system that taught me was extending the opportunity for me to be able to do the same for the students at Southern at Baton Rouge and Southern at Shreveport.

This upcoming fall will be my fourth year as a professor at Southern. Many of my students I taught my first year will now become seniors. The love I have for my knowledge in history, and how I teach and present it to my students, is an art. One that I must give credit to Southern University for helping me find the art and apply it. I tell my students all the time, "If you can make it here at Southern, there is nothing you won't be ready for. The world is yours!"

About Shala Washington

Shala is a professor of history, doctoral student, community leader, youth basketball organizer, entrEpreneur, wife, and mother.

Shala Washington is a native of Augusta, Georgia but due to her father joining the Army when she was five years old, she moved around a lot during her earlier years. She stayed in Georgia until she was fifteen years old, when her dad was stationed to Ft. Hood, Texas. A graduate of Killeen High in 2008, her next move was starting college in Baton Rouge, Louisiana at Southern University A&M.

Always a lover of history, her professors at Southern taught her and helped mentor her to become the professor she is today. Her love for history and her passion to teach the youth became her another heart outside of her body. Her new business, Professor Lai, is a historical consultation firm that specializes in consults of all historic nature, content, background, research, and data. Her main purpose of starting Professor Lai, is to promote, encourage, and teach history from a bright, new, and understanding perspective.

Shala met her husband in 2009, while in her spring semester of her freshman year. They dated and wed in July 2015, while Shala was in her first year of graduate school. Almost immediately after the wedding, she was pregnant with her first child. Unfortunately, five months into her pregnancy, a complication took over her body and the only way to save her life, was to deliver the baby. By delivering the baby at twenty-one weeks, he passed away, and it pushed Shala into a state of depression. Her and her husband had to overcome a traumatic situation at only seven months into their marriage. This pushed them closer together and was the push to start their local youth basketball organization, the Baton Rouge 6ers. By founding an organization with family members, with the same common goal in mind, has helped make their organization one of the biggest in the Baton Rouge area. The Baton Rouge 6ers, is an organization and basketball family that is for young boys and girls, ages 3-14. With sports being a major part of the inner-city community of Baton Rouge, the organization serves as a major part of the community for many boys, girls, and families.

Her love and passion for the youth and fashion combined with being a mother of three black children, inspired her to create an online children's boutique, with her children being co-owners as well. Shala believes that representation means a lot, especially for children, which is one of the driving factors of the business. She also is an event planner and decorator of Lavish Events LA, which she branched from her parent's business, Lavish Events in Georgia. Children's parties and brunches are her favorite events to set up.

During undergrad at Southern, Shala received her B.A. in history. She took a year off school, then went back to get her Master of Social Science with a concentration in history. After becoming a mother and starting her dream job of a professor, Shala knew she had to take her professional career to another height. At the start of the pandemic, she started her doctoral program in philosophy with a concentration in history with her kids and her being home almost 24/7. She committed herself to this major step before knowing what was in store for the year of 2020, but she stayed focus and dedicated to the main goal.

Briana C. Spivey, Esq.

A Second Chance for a Better Investment
Briana C. Spivey, Esq.

"Who taught you to hate yourself?"

This question that Malcom X posed to an audience is the same question that came to mind as I prepared to write this chapter. When asked to participate in this project, I was honored once I got over the initial intimidation. I reflected on my time at Southern University Law Center, and how the decision to attend literally changed my life. I felt a sense of guilt and wished I would have considered attending an HBCU early.

There were problematic narratives that I remember hearing as I contemplated what undergraduate school to attend. The narratives were that HBCUs wouldn't prepare you for the "real" world. HBCUs wouldn't be as challenging. Both of those narratives were not true. But they led me to make one of the biggest mistakes of my life: not even considering attending an HBCU for undergrad. The worst part of this is I don't remember where I originally heard this or why I was convinced it was true. However, as I realized I wanted to go to law school, I was fortunate enough to get another chance to consider, apply and get accepted, attend and graduate from an HBCU law school (1/6 of the only HBCU law programs).

When I decided I wanted to go to law school, Southern University Law Center stood out to me as one of the best law schools I could attend in Louisiana. Southern University had a reputation for having a great law program and producing quality attorneys. Southern University Law Center was my first choice. With the help of my cousin, and a man by the name of Ernest Nabors, I was able to begin a life-changing journey. When I first applied, I didn't have stellar grades or a stellar LSAT score, but they still chose to invest in me. The interim chancellor, admissions faculty and staff, and recruiting professors all saw beyond my fears. They saw me as good enough and they chose to invest in me, all before I even paid a seat deposit to attend school.

I felt like my LSAT score would never be high enough to be admitted, but they referred me to an LSAT program that on campus.

Because of that, I was able to score enough to be admitted. I felt like I wouldn't be ready to attend law school when I first found out I got accepted. The interim chancellor referred me to a one-week pre-law program to help me feel more comfortable since I would not be able to attend the pre-law program at the school. I trusted them with my life, and it was one of the best decisions I've ever made.

Attending Southern for law school debunked every falsehood I had ever heard about HBCUs. The curriculum was challenging. We were prepared for the real world, especially during 1L year. Our professors were adamant about us learning and doing things ourselves because that information would not always be readily available in the real world/practice of law. However, they were in tune with the needs of their students. They took their time to teach and help us when it became clear we would not be able to do so ourselves. Now that I am a practicing attorney, I appreciate that most. I am not intimidated when I don't readily know the answer to a question or have the solution to a problem. I am also confident in my abilities because, just like before, if I am unable to handle a problem on my own, I know that I can reach out to other professors/ alumni for help, after trying on my own first, of course. This, too, was great preparation for the real world in the practice of law. Our motto, "Seriousness of Purpose" was instilled in us. We all have a purpose. Being at SULC, I was able to discover my purpose and sharpen the skills necessary to walk in my purpose.

Attending Southern was both an academic and a social culture shock. I realized that all of those negative things I was told were simply not true. I had never experienced a homecoming where musical artists from all backgrounds come to perform for the students. Even our annual formal, also known as the Barrister's Ball, had all of the formalities one would experience at any other law school formal. It still managed to be one of the most fun events I have ever attended. There was the usual pomp and circumstance, but it was never boring. Gatherings on the bluff with other students felt no different than gatherings with family and friends.

I had never been surrounded by so many people who looked like me. I experienced freedom to be myself and express myself in a way where I was culturally understood. While I did have to maintain professionalism, there was not a need for such strict internal policing amongst my peers. I did not realize it at the time, but this too was another luxury I was afforded by attending an HBCU. Another luxury I took for granted was the ability to see potential in our professors. Whether I wanted to be an attorney, mediator, politician, legislator, commissioner, judge, or even news correspondent, I saw it in the halls of SULC. Any program we had on campus came with the opportunity to network and learn information that would make students more well-rounded. Not only was I able to see what's possible for myself career-wise, but I was also able to see what was possible for my legacy. With every step I took to become an attorney, I felt the support of fellow professors, classmates, faculty and other alumni one thousand percent. Alumni helped me prepare for the bar exam and even awarded me a scholarship to cover the cost of taking the exam.

Countless times, I was extended grace. HBCUs take students and invest in them. When you invest in HBCUs, you help them invest in their students. HBCUs mold students into people like no other school setting would be able to do. They are an invaluable resource for Black talent and Black culture. They are filled with history, tradition and pride that is so rich that it inspires not only its students, but the world. I learned that if you do not take time to learn the truth about yourself, it will be easy to believe someone else's lies about you. So, in closing, my message to the world is that if HBCU culture is good enough for films, TV shows and performances, HBCU curriculums need to be good enough for enrollment, grants and resources. I trusted them with my life and, as a result of that decision, I am a practicing attorney today.

About Briana C. Spivey, Esq.

Briana Camille Spivey was born in West Monroe, Louisiana to Gwendolyn Spivey and the late Bob Spivey. She graduated from the University of Louisiana at Lafayette with a major in Political Science, concentrating in Pre-Law, and minor in Public Relations. Throughout her matriculation at Southern University Law Center, she has interned at the East Baton Rouge Public Defender's Office, at the 19th JDC for the Honorable Donald Johnson, and at the 19th JDC for the Honorable Trudy White.

While in Law School she has been a part of Women in Law, Black Law Students Association, and has served as Campaign Manager for numerous Student Bar Association Candidates. During her last semester, Briana has worked as a teaching assistant for first year family law students, interned at the 19th JDC under Judge White, volunteered for a judicial campaign, all while going to school full time and making the Dean's List. Although hesitant about coming to law school, Briana has learned how to study the law and even learned to love the law. She considers the lessons she's learned about herself to be some of the greatest lessons she has learned since coming to law school. Upon graduation, Briana worked in Lafayette, La as an intern at a local law firm. Briana passed the February 2020 bar exam, and began practicing as a children in need of care attorney.

She serves on the Children's Law and Outreach committees of the Louisiana Bar Association; and is a member of the Monroe chapters of the Martinet Society and the NAACP.

Kevin L. Lopez, M.A., RSW

Statistic Turned Scholar
Kevin L. Lopez, M.A., RSW

One of the best decisions I made in life was listening to one of my best friends while working at Walgreens. I applied with him to Southern University at New Orleans. I struggled heavily as a high school student, as well as at the community college. It goes without saying that college was definitely not the first thing on my mind.

Coming from the upbringing that I had, it was no secret that I was more interested in fast money than I was in obtaining good grades. While family members stepped in and tried to correct these issues, and put more of an importance on education, I had an obligation to assist my family as much as possible. It was not until a series of unfortunate events that I honestly decided to take my education seriously. I was partaking in a lot of high-risk behavior. A quick reality check gave me all the reason I needed to heed my best friend's advice and apply to college, specifically Southern University at New Orleans.

I knew that the road I was going down would be nothing short of detrimental to, not only myself, but my family, as well. Three weeks before classes began, I had still yet to hear from the university about my application. My best friend had already received his approval letter. Deadlines were approaching fast, and I was desperate. I was either going to be packing up my things and moving to a new state, or I was going to stay put where I was in Texas and fall into the same cycle of behaviors that had gotten me where I was in that moment. How could I be so upset about something that I continuously told myself meant so little? Who was I to think that any university would take a chance on me? Why should they?

That very next morning, I woke up and decided that maybe college just wasn't for me. However, while I sat, I could feel myself get discouraged and sad. I wanted to do better. I wanted to be better. I went to have breakfast with my grandparents, as I normally did on my days off from work. Sitting right on the counter was a letter from Southern University at New Orleans. My heart dropped. After all the waiting, the time was finally here. It did not seem real. I ripped open the envelope. In bold lettering, the first words my eyes saw were, "Congratulations, you have been accepted!" I was officially a college student, and I could not have been more ecstatic.

The college experience was all new to me. I did not know what I wanted to major in. I just knew I would not be leaving until I got my bachelor's degree in something. Transitioning from the mess I had created during my time in community college was rough. Things quickly picked up. I thought I found my niche at the university with psychology, so that was my major. I had always known that I wanted to help people. What better way to do that than to try and understand the way that individuals think? While I definitely enjoyed learning about the psychology of people, something was missing. I just didn't know what it was. I was interested, but the excitement was sort of wearing off. I thought I was lost again.

The next semester, my first summer term, I ended up registering for a social work course to complete my elective requirement for the psychology degree. This was one of the most important decisions of my life. Social work was my calling, and it did not take me long to realize it. I had found a drive for school that I didn't even know existed. I woke up the very next morning and walked from my dorm to the admissions office. I put in a request and switched my major.

After my first two semesters attending Southern University at New Orleans, it was clear that the university was not as valued as much as some of the other universities in the city. The assumption from locals was that the university was like a high school extension. No one willingly applied or even thought of attending. This could not be further from the truth. Southern University at New Orleans was my saving grace. I am not sure that I would be in the position I am today without the lessons learned from the university. Southern University at New Orleans molded me into the individual I am today. I was lost at one point in life. I didn't think I would amount to anything more than a statistic. However, Southern University at New Orleans gave me an opportunity to change for the better.

Due to Southern University at New Orleans taking that chance on me, I now know what my life's purpose is. I have an amazing career in doing what I love. The stigma of Southern University at

New Orleans being a "bottom of the barrel" university is a falsehood that I work diligently to change. I've witnessed social workers from other universities, big name universities, from the state of Louisiana crumble under pressure. They are not able to relate to or adapt to the population that social workers serve in the community. They normally end up changing career paths. Social work is not an easy occupation, but the education and training that I was able to receive at Southern University at New Orleans gave me leverage over everyone else. Attending an HBCU over a predominantly white institution will help advance you as an individual not just in your career but in life. I started my journey only wanting to accomplish the minimum, a bachelor's degree. Almost eight years later, I am currently working on a PhD. It all started with Southern University at New Orleans.

Attending Southern University at New Orleans was a blessing for me. I have been successful in my career thus far. When individuals ask, "Where did you go to school" I state my university proudly. I have been, and I continue to sit, in meetings where people look at me differently because of where I obtained my degree. But the gag is that I am usually their boss or the most qualified person sitting in the meeting. So, while others may have their own personal views of what an HBCU is, or even what Southern University at New Orleans is, I am a proud alumnus. I demand my respect, as well as the respect for my beloved Southern University at New Orleans.

About Kevin L. Lopez, M.A., RSW

Kevin Lopez was raised in Queens, New York up until his teenage years when his family then moved to Mesquite, Texas. As a young adult Kevin always knew he wanted to help people, he just needed clarity on how to accomplish that. Kevin is the eldest of four and takes pride in being a positive example for his younger brothers. After some tough life lessons, Kevin made the decision to take a chance on himself and try to accomplish something that has never been done in his family, which was to attend a university.

Southern University at New Orleans School of social work program seemed to be exactly what Kevin was looking for. Kevin found an admiration for social work and was able to matriculate through the program confidently. Kevin was interested in continuing his education past his Bachelor's degree and went on to obtain his Masters degree in Criminal Justice. Kevin associated being able to utilize his Social work skills to better connect with the juvenile individuals partaking in high-risk behavior just as he once had done. Kevin is now outperforming his own personal goal and is currently working towards his P. HD.

Kevin now works directly within the New Orleans metropolitan at a grassroots organization, Louisiana Council of Resources, where he is able to maximize his experiences and expertise advocating for those who can not advocate for themselves. Kevin quickly became a Mental Health advocate and sits on a number of community coalition groups determined to help positively change the Criminal Justice system. Kevin is committed to becoming the best version of himself while helping as many people as he can on the way.

To learn more about Kevin Lopez, got to www.kevinllopez.com.

Kia Bickham

My Roots Run Deep; My Pride Runs Deeper!
Kia Bickham

Growing up, I never realized the impact Southern University would have on my life. From an early age, I was exposed to all of what Southern University is, was and what it will continue to be. My parents, and the rest of my support system, taught me the history and exposed me to the university.

Sitting in the cold, drinking hot chocolate in A.W. Mumford Stadium, traveling to away football games, campaigning with political leaders, helping my cousins move in and out of Boley and Octavia Halls, and watching in awe as The Human Jukebox and Fabulous Dancing Dolls marched through the streets of New Orleans during Mardi Gras gave me great joy. I knew, one day, I would be a Southern Jaguar.

While in high school, I entertained the options of going to an out-of-state institution. I thought Southern University and A&M College was too familiar, would prohibit growth opportunities, and would not allow me to expand my tentacles. The Louisiana Taylor Opportunity Program for Students (TOPS) was an initiative that provided scholarships for Louisiana residents who planned on attending one of Louisiana's public colleges or universities. This seemed to be a resolution that would offer me the comfort of being homebased, as well as, affordability options. After comprehensive discussions and considerations with my family, I realized the economic impact and the advantages of remaining true to my heart was possibly at my fingertips. After much contemplation and giving in to my inner voices, Southern University was my final answer, without question.

My Southern University experience surely didn't disappoint. One of my first memories as a freshman, in the Fall of 1998, was ambulating through the doors of the John B. Cade library to make the journey upstairs to the Honors College to select my classes. I was greeted by a vivacious, feisty woman who I later realized was the dean of the Honors College, Dr. Beverly Dixon Wade. My first encounter with Dean Wade set the tone for my time at Southern and for my life's journey. She emphasized the importance of being prepared, asking questions for clarity, and excellence being the only option.

I encountered professors and administrators who exemplified the same values as Dean Wade throughout my time as an undergraduate student. I later learned that was Southern University's philosophy. We were taught to always be the best. We were taught that, as African Americans, we always have to outperform our White counterparts in the real world. The professors instilled in us that, with a Southern University education, one could succeed anywhere. The world was ours, as students, to conquer.

I also realized that Southern had a diverse curriculum and extracurricular activities to meet the needs for most students. My interest in journalism and photography landed me a spot on the Southern University Digest staff as a photographer and reporter. I carried around my dad's Canon 35-mm camera daily, capturing Southern University life and completing assignments as directed by the editorial team. When I joined the staff, it was a time of turmoil and rebuilding. Limited resources existed and the priority to provide equipment for the staff had not been established. My personal camera offered easy access to join the team!

As a freshman, in order to earn your stripes, you had to perform the indistinguishable tasks. I distinctly remember one of my first assignments. The hot topic that semester was a professor who allegedly threw a desk at a student. Our editorial team wanted to cover it, but they were somewhat hesitant. They ultimately decided that we would move forward, and I was assigned to get a photo of the professor teaching to accompany the story. The professor's class happened to be a few doors from the Digest office on the second floor of Harris Hall. My assignment was clear: Get in and out quickly to get the shot without the professor noticing. I put on a baseball cap, turned it backwards, grabbed my backpack and camera, and started down the hall. I passed by the class and noticed several familiar faces that I knew would blow my cover. I tried to tell them to act normal so I wouldn't alert the professor. That plan didn't work.

As I eased into the classroom, they immediately started

laughing, which alerted the professor. I held my camera up and began shooting. I tried my best to get a good shot, but the professor was infuriated and started yelling at me. I backed out of the room and proceeded to run down the hall back to the Digest office, with the professor several steps behind me. As soon as I got in the office, I threw the baseball cap on the floor, dropped my backpack and hid my camera in the desk drawer. My editor at the time knew what happened because he was watching from the door. So, as soon as the professor tried to enter the office, he ran interference and tried to convince the professor that the story he described did not happen. However, my lime green backpack was in plain sight. That was the evidence that he cited to call our bluff. We were not able to use the photo because of the professor's objection, but the experience was definitely memorable. Most importantly, I got the shot.

My journey with the Digest took off from there. I received better assignments, and, by my sophomore year, I was named the photo editor for the Digest. I simultaneously became the editor of the Jaguar Yearbook, returning it to a yearly production after a three-year hiatus. As the editor-in-chief, I traveled with the football team and served on the press team for the Essence Music Festival. It opened the door to many new opportunities. During my tenure, we were able to upgrade our technology and we purchased Apple computers for the student media teams.

In the Fall of 2000, I was initiated into the Beta Psi chapter of Alpha Kappa Alpha Sorority, Incorporated. The experience was rewarding yet challenging, but it provided memories that I will carry with me for a lifetime. I gained sisters, a network of mentors, and women who continue to have an impact on my life today.

My matriculation at Southern was like none other. I received a bachelor's degree in Mass Communications in the Spring of 2002. I felt prepared as I entered the workforce, but I wanted to continue my education as I embarked on a career in politics. I returned to Southern in the Fall of 2005, and I received my master's in public administration in the Spring of 2008.

At Southern, I met friends who became family. I learned many lessons, like patience, how to make a way out of no way, and how not to take "no" for an answer. When I graduated, I felt compelled to give back to a place that gave so much to me.

I am an active member of the SU Alumni Federation. I previously served as a local chapter president and set the foundation for the chapter to grow from ten members to over 230 members currently. I am also a member of the Southern University System Foundation's 1880 Society, where members are expected to reach a minimum yearly philanthropic contribution.

Historical Black Colleges and Universities (HBCUs) are the backbone for Black culture and advancement. I learned through my education in predominantly white environments, as a child, that people felt institutions like Southern University are inferior to predominantly white institutions. I am thankful for my tribe that taught me and demonstrated otherwise.

It's not a secret that, historically, our institutions have been severely under-resourced and have been able to make tremendous contributions, in spite of our circumstances. It is incumbent upon HBCU grads to keep the legacy of our institutions alive. We can't expect others to support us when we don't support ourselves. Many of us would not be where we are without Southern University. We should, especially as alums, be forever grateful and show our appreciation to the institution that gave so much to us.

Southern University graduates dominate and contribute to society globally. My Southern University experience has afforded me the opportunity to serve two governors, a lieutenant governor, two mayors and a member of Congress. Therefore, I make a conscience effort to help open the doors for other Jaguars to help keep our legacy alive.

To paraphrase our Alma Mater...

"O Southern, Dear Southern, thy praises we shall sing...

O Southern, Dear Southern, we owe our all to thee..."

About Kia Bickham

Kia Bickham is highly-motivated, self-directed, and results-oriented strategic community engagement specialist with over 15 years of experience, an extensive network of contacts at the local, state, and federal level and skilled at collaborating with members of the executive and legislative branches of municipal and state government and key stakeholder groups.

Kia currently serves as the Director of Engagement for E Pluribus Unum, a nonprofit organization that focuses on building a more just, inclusive, and equitable South through advancing social change and racial equity. She is also the managing partner of KDB Strategies, LLC where she specializes in strategic community engagement consulting. Prior to beginning her own consulting firm, she served as the political director for the Adrian Perkins for US Senate campaign, Mike Bloomberg presidential campaign in Louisiana and as the political director for the Campaign to Re-Elect Governor John Bel Edwards, where she worked tirelessly to develop and implement a strategic voter engagement plan. With her assistance, Governor John Bel Edwards was re-elected to serve a second term. She also served as a community outreach and project manager for APTIM Environmental and Infrastructure, Inc., a leading global provider of program management, energy efficiency programs, integrated maintenance services, environmental engineering and remediation, and disaster response and recovery for private sector and government clients. In her role with Aptim, Kia specialized in effective communication and relationship building strategies with demonstrated success in programmatic, operational, logistical and managerial support.

Ms. Bickham has an extensive background in community and civic engagement, serving as the Chief Service Officer for the City of Baton Rouge under Mayor-President Melvin L. "Kip" Holden for six years until her transition to the private sector in 2017. As Chief Service Officer, she managed citizen-led volunteer engagement initiatives to address the city's most pressing challenges such as neighborhood revitalization and youth development.

During her tenure with the City of Baton Rouge, the citizen-led neighborhood revitalization projects resulted in the transformation of approximately 30 neighborhood blocks and 69 vacant lots, the collection and disposal of more almost 3 tons of litter, the installation of numerous energy-efficiency home improvements to help low-income residents reduce energy use and lower their energy costs, and the engagement of more than 3,000 volunteers to perform more than 8,000 volunteers hours for the Baton Rouge community.

Her most notable accomplishment during her tenure with the City was designing and implementing the "Love Our Community" neighborhood revitalization and environmental stewardship summer youth employment program. Between 2013 and 2016, the program under her leadership provided more than 500 youth between the ages of 14-25 with an opportunity to earn income while completing work that benefited themselves, the environment and the community. Program participants built and maintained community gardens and green spaces, fought blight through mural arts and public art projects, and participated in numerous educational and professional development trainings.

Prior to joining Mayor Holden's team, she served in various consulting capacities including political campaigns and as a project manager for Hilton Hotels & Resorts. She also served as a Community Outreach Manager for the Office of Lieutenant Governor Mitch Landrieu and Executive Assistant to the Deputy Chief of Staff and Policy Director for the late Governor Kathleen Babineaux Blanco.

She is extremely active in her community with memberships in a variety of organizations. She currently serves as an investment team leader for the Capital Area United Way, and is a member of the board of directors for Serve Louisiana and BASIS Baton Rouge, a local charter school. She is also a member of Alpha Kappa Alpha Sorority, Inc.

Her experience has also afforded her the opportunity to receive additional academic training from the Loyola Institute of Politics, the Louisiana State University Academy of Applied Politics and the Cornell University High Performance Leadership Program. In 2014, she was recognized by the Baton Rouge Business Report as one of the area's Top 40 Under Forty and received the same honor from the Southern University Alumni Federation in 2019. She was also a 2020 Esprit de Femme award winner from the Louisiana State University Women's Center for her exceptional efforts to assuage the struggles of women in her community, state and culture.

She earned a Masters in Public Administration from Southern University and A&M College (2008), where she also earned a Bachelor of Arts in Mass Communications (2002). While at Southern University, she was privileged to work as a writer and photographer for the Southern University Digest. But her proudest moment was when she was named Editor-In-Chief of the Millennium Edition of the Jaguar Yearbook (1999-2000) as a sophomore and successfully returned the yearbook to a yearly production after a three year hiatus.

She is proud to say that she bleeds blue and gold and is devoted to working with individuals and organizations committed to preserving the Southern University legacy. She served as president of the Southern University Alumni Home Chapter, a member of the Southern University Alumni Federation and the Southern University System Foundation's 1880 Society. She was also instrumental in the engagement of the young alumni movement, which has now formalized itself as the Southern University Young Alumni Network.

Bambi Dupree-Alridge

And the Band Played On
Bambi Dupree-Alridge

From the time I was a little girl, I loved watching the Southern University Marching Band. I was born into a musical family, and I started my career in music as a singer at the age of four. Every summer, my cousins and I boarded a train and headed to Chicago, where music was plentiful. Artistically educated between New Orleans and Chicago, I brought a wealth of knowledge and performance experience. Every November, The Bayou Classic located in New Orleans brings people from all over the country. My first game blew my mind. It forever changed my musical life.

My neighborhood was made up of residents who attended, or were attending, an HBCU. Southern University was heavily represented. Growing up in an area where African American teachers and principals were of great abundance, my education was filled with representatives of HBCUs. Music has always been my lifeline and source of sustainability. So, entering college and matriculating in music was no surprise.

I entered the campus of Southern University in the early 80s assigned to Boley Hall. Seventeen and ready to take on the world, I ran into two young ladies from my hometown. They arrived earlier than I, and the suite they were assigned to was already filled. Initially, I thought this was the worst thing that could happen, until I met my suitemates. At face value, we were a motley crew. But we were all especially gifted in our own ways. Eight young ladies were thrown together in one suite, with only two having any knowledge of one another. It wasn't long before we were making group dinners together, hotplates all ablaze, heavenly aromas filling the air/ hallways and music blasting.

The first week on campus is amazing for freshmen. It's an opportunity to learn your way around campus before upperclassmen return to claim their turf. Most importantly, the upperclassmen band members also returned to campus. Residents, graduate band members and freshmen all would walk or drive over to the band practice field to listen and watch what we all affectionately called

"The Human Jukebox" practice. The Southern University Band has both a cult and groupie following. You would run into young ladies who looked totally unlike musicians, as they made their way down the hall to stand in the doorway of band hall. When band practice started, you could turn off your radio and listen to the band playing the same Top 20 you hear on the radio.

If you knew anything at all about the marching band, you knew it was a "No Females" club. This always perplexed my mind because the other HBCUs had females in their bands. After getting my first semester out the way, a few of the female music majors asked if I played any instruments. I was invited to play in the concert band and possibly rush into the band sorority. I was caught off guard since I was a music major, I sang in the concert choir and women's choir, yet I never saw one female in the band. I drove home over the weekend and returned with my instrument. I wasn't sure how females would be received in "the" band.

The band hall was filled with instrumentalists warming up until rehearsals began. Concert band turned out to be where the rubber met the road. It separated musicianship from the instrument players. Music sheets were passed around and we had to read what was placed before us. We couldn't pretend to put our instrument together slowly until we caught on by ear. We had to know how to read music. The band hall went from standing room only to getting a seat at-will. Concert band was both enriching and rewarding, which led me to pledge Tau Beta Sigma (band sorority). I built lifelong relationships through Tau Beta Sigma, and I pledged with line brothers who would become members of Kappa Kappa Psi (band fraternity). Never in my wildest dreams would I ever think that talking over joining the marching band with sorority sisters would turn out to be a solo endeavor. The first year of college came to an end. I told the group I would see them during Crab Week. This is when all freshmen or new members show up to try out for marching band.

Prior to leaving home, I found it difficult to get in touch with the other females who were meeting for tryouts. All incoming students living on campus reported to the freshmen dorms. I headed back to Boley Hall. I was informed that no room had been reserved for me to stay in during tryout week. I headed to the band hall. I went into the office and asked to speak with Doc regarding my dorm assignment. I was politely informed that while I was free to try out for the band, there would not be any special privileges made on my part. The South Louisiana girl came out in me.

"I don't think asking for a room is a special privilege since all the boys have a dorm room."

I shook that first obstacle off by procuring a place to stay with one of my Tau Beta Sigma sorority sisters. It was going to be a hassle having to get up earlier than the guys, not having a place to relax during the day while going through tryouts, and still having to drive home after late-night rehearsals. But I said I would try. Try is what I did.

Allow me to paint a picture of what not getting special privileges meant regarding marching band tryouts. It meant that I didn't get housing, so I started my new day tired from the previous day. While we all had an equal number of laps to run, mine came with a new and fresh upperclassman at every lap. I had to run at their pace, not that of my own. My crab brothers were penalized if caught giving any support. Many hoped this would make me throw in the towel. The word that a young lady was at tryouts, and doing well, got out. Reporters came out to watch this female doing it alone.

The last day of tryouts, everyone was on edge. The press was gnawing at Doc, and his wife was pleading with him to just let it go. Doc called me in and told me, "Even if you make it through this week, you're never going to march on the field." I just smiled, unpacked my trombone and headed to get into line to march to the practice field. As usual, I got the non-privileged special treatment of running a race instead of running to warm up. On the fifth turn, I pulled a muscle and headed to the infirmary. Crying all the way there, and the entire time I was getting treatment, all I could think of was, *This is it. I've blown my chance at showing Doc something different.* I packed up my horn after returning and finished out the day. Not one word was said as to whether I'd made it or not. I left feeling accomplished, but not fulfilled.

Every cloud has a silver lining. My *her*story of making the band holds a place all by itself. I made the city and school papers, but Doc did have the final say. My name is Bambi Dupree-Alridge, and I was the first female to break the glass ceiling of the Southern University Marching Band. I was also the first female to make the band. But I never had a chance to suit up or march on the field. Does that make me a failure? Not in the least bit. I created the blueprint for females to not only make the band, but march on the field.

The Human Jukebox now has young ladies … and the band still plays on!

About Bambi Dupree-Alridge

Bambi Dupree-Alridge is a retired Opera/Classical Singer, Minister, Activist, Spirit Healer and the Founder of Love In Full Enlightenment (L.I.F.E.), a healing organization that promotes bringing forth authenticity and freedom living.

Bambi was born in Houma, LA and currently resides in Indianapolis, IN with her beautiful wife Kim, where she continues to do activism and racial healing. Bambi has been shattering glass ceilings for a very long time and has no intentions of stopping anytime soon.

Shametria Gonzales

Survival Over Success
Shametria Gonzales

I was in ninth grade when a man came to my school and gave us a presentation on how to get into college and choose our major. He sparked our imagination. I never knew about college or how I could get there until I heard that man speak. From that day forward, I started on the path to get scholarships. I knew I didn't have any money and I had truly little support. But learning about FASFA and scholarships changed my perception. No one in my family had been to college before. I was just a small-town, country girl at heart.

I knew I wanted to attend an HBCU because my high school was 90% Caucasian. I wanted to experience the stuff I saw on TV when I watched the battle of the bands, like on *Drumline*. Four years after I heard that man speak, my dream finally came true. I passed my exit exams, took my ACT, and received a full scholarship to college. I was eighteen when I came to SUNO. I had over twelve scholarship offers to play ball, but SUNO was my best pick because of the atmosphere and the fact that they offered me a full ride. I was recruited by Coach King to play basketball! This changed my life forever. It's pulled me from a life of instability and living from place to place to being a collegiate athlete.

I was a small-town teen who came from a troubled background. But that one opportunity to go to college changed everything for me. It was a new beginning. I didn't have a typical childhood. I went to over twenty schools since I was seven years old. I never stayed with one family member for too long before I was on to the next home. As I walked into my apartments at SUNO for the first time, I knew my life would never be the same. I knew it was the beginning of the rest of my life. I never knew what the Black experience meant. But when I stepped on campus, I saw people from all over the world. I saw people who looked like me and that shared my experience. SUNO provided stability and a family atmosphere for me and my one-year-old daughter like we'd never felt before.

Since I came from a small town and graduated from God's Academy in Texas, the New Orleans atmosphere was like nothing

I'd ever experienced. My classmates were so close, and everyone knew each other. The whole school came to watch our games and support us. Although I was there to play basketball, I was so glad they asked me to join the volleyball team. The coach said she loved my energy and how I used my voice to spark the other players. I was not that good at volleyball or basketball my first year, but I had heart and a good work ethic. I had nothing to lose and no home to go back to. I could not fail at college or lose my scholarship.

Most kids go to school to learn how to do something that will make them money in the long run. They go to college to further their education. They go to college to live out their dreams. They go to college for the experience. Not me! I went to college for *survival*! All I knew was if I passed my classes, I would get to play sports. If I played sports, I would get to keep my scholarship. As long as I kept my scholarship, I would get to have three meals a day and a place for me and my daughter to lay our heads! It was hard and it was a struggle. But our coach went above and beyond and made sure we kept good grades. Coach always made sure that we carried ourselves with respect.

I was a woman of faith and, although I was troubled, I suppressed my pain and turned that into purpose. I encourage anyone reading this book to always remember that it's not about how you start; it's about how you finish. It was hard. I wanted to quit and go home so many times. Instead, I kept showing up and doing my best. You're a winner as long as you don't quit. During my five years at SUNO, I learned how to be a woman. One time after my freshman year, I was worried that I would not get a chance to come back. Coach King decided not to give me a scholarship for basketball the second year. I was crying and packing my stuff to leave when my friend Zipporaha came to my room and chewed me out. She told me not to give up. She told me to go to summer schools and get the credit I needed to be able to play volleyball because they needed me on the team that year. Although I lost my basketball scholarship, I had one chance left to keep my volleyball scholarship.

Thank God I listened. Everything changed after that. I went to tryouts and I made the team. I went to summer school and got all the credits I needed to be eligible for the next school year. I got a mentor and I figured out my classes. I got a job at a local hair shop. I finally took school seriously. I never looked back. I changed my name from NaeNae to Shametria. I became the woman I am today that day. From then on, everything was smooth sailing. Each year after that, I passed my classes. I became ranked in conference for volleyball, and I started on the journey of self-development and self-mastery.

After I finished college, I was not sure what to do with my life. But God's plans were right on time. I started off my career working for the Family Justice Center of New Orleans. From there, I branched off into motivational speaking. I became an author, a business owner and a state contractor. Today, I work as a community organizer for the Justice and Accountability Center of Louisiana. I created a reentry program for women called the F.O.R.W.A.R.D. movement. It stands for Focused On Real Women And Real Dreams. We pair women who have been released from jail with leaders in the community in order to make sure they have a smooth transition into society.

Me and my daughter coauthored a book called *The Reflection Eyes See*. It focuses on how to heal from past traumas and look at yourself through a different lens. Last year, our organization passed over seven new laws revolving around criminal justice reform. Pretty soon, I may even use the skills and knowledge I gained from SUNO to run for office.

I consider myself a servant leader. The only reason I am the woman you see today is because of everything I learned and experienced at SUNO. Everyone who graduated from SUNO is a part of the change that's going on in New Orleans today. We have a proud culture at SUNO. We all came out to watch and support our Greek life on campus. This was one of my favorite things to do. I was too busy with sports to pledge, but that's still one of my dreams. Another experience that I remember is when they tried to merge SUNi with UNO. We marched side by side with poster boards and megaphones, begging the funders to remember the history of SUNO. Due to those efforts and the support of our community leaders, SUNO is still standing solo today.

If you went to SUNO between 2010 and 2015, you can't help but remember the legacy of the family culture and love we had for each other. Ultimately, I am still friends with all the same people I met during college. I would not change my experience of going to SUNO for the world. I see SUNO graduates who are lawyers, social workers, state politicians, community leaders and business owners. I am about to turn thirty years old, and I have no regrets. I encourage everyone reading my story to always remember that if there is no enemy within, the enemy outside can do you no harm. Always believe in yourself and your dreams. Your life matters. Your story matters. Together, we can be the change that sparks the world to change!

About Shametria Gonzales

Shametria Gonzales is JAC's Community Organizer. She hosts the Louisiana Stop Solitary Coalition and works with the Clean Slate Coalition to stop solitary confinement and automate expungements in the state of Louisiana.

Shametria conducts outreach to formerly incarcerated individuals and their families and connects individuals impacted by the criminal system with policymakers to advocate for change. She is also the Founder of the FORWARD reentry project assisting women that have recently been released from prison to connect with resources, mentorship, and advocacy during their transition back into society. Shametria believes working to end solitary confinement and to automate expungements in the state of Louisiana will be the start of a long line of advocacy work for her career as a servant leader.

Shametria is an educator, presenter, and activist on issues of trauma. She is the founder of Spiritually Connected, an organization that helps women and children redevelop themselves after experiencing trauma. Prior to joining JAC, Shemetria worked as a Rape Prevention Educator for the New Orleans Family Justice Center, was a facilitator for the Teen Sex and the Law program for the Children's Advocacy Center, and a Medical Advocate for University Hospital where she assisted victims of sexual assault. Shametria co-authored a book with her nine-year old daughter, *The Reflection Eyes See*, to raise awareness on the effects of childhood trauma.

Mieké J. Hampton, M.S.

Black Excellence
Mieké J. Hampton, M.S.

Attending an HBCU has always been my dream. I have been blessed to have the option to attend any predominantly white institution or Ivy League school. However, the schools at the top of my list were always historically black colleges and universities (HBCUs): Howard University, Clark Atlanta, Spelman, and of course, Southern University and Agricultural and Mechanical College. Southern University has always been the school most talked about in my family. From attending the tailgates and games as a child, to being enrolled in Upward Bound and Educational Talent Search, I was reared in true blue and gold fashion. My summers and weekends were spent on the campus of Southern University for various programs.

Recently, during my trip home to pick up my daughter during the pandemic, I rummaged through some old schoolwork from both my primary and secondary education. Every now and then in elementary school, students are charged with the task of writing about what they would like to be when they grow up. Well, undoubtedly, I wanted to go to Southern University, and I wanted to become a doctor. My family legacy, coupled with my overwhelming love for Southern, made attending this institution an effortless choice. In middle school, a similar essay prompt was requested by an English teacher. In my paper, I wrote, "I am going to go to Southern University to get my Bachelor's in Microbiology, then go back to get my Master's, then go to medical school to become a doctor. After that, I plan to open chains of hospitals in underserved communities in the south." That middle school girl from small town White Castle, Louisiana spoke her dreams with such conviction.

In high school, the seniors in our school district were charged with the task of creating a senior project. Of course, this encompasses a thorough, professionally written paper, job shadowing, and integration of skills taught through our tenure in high school to be presented to judges. Let's jump into the paper. This time, my paper detailed exactly how I was going to reach my goal of becoming a doctor. What did that goal start with? Attending Southern University. What I was most sure about was that, in for me to become a doctor, I needed to attend an HBCU. The HBCU most engrained in my blood and etched in my heart was none other than the prestigious Southern University and A&M College. My aunt attended SU and rocked out. She has always been, and still is, one of my role models. As a child, I was taught the importance of attending an HBCU early on.

Most students attending an HBCU soon come into a sense of belonging, pride and heritage. That was not my story. I already had all those things. Growing up in a small community, and attending a predominately black elementary and high school, I never felt "out of place". I was always seen and welcomed. However, stepping foot on the campus of Southern University as a freshman student in 2008, the sense of belonging, pride and heritage was enhanced. I soaked up the cultural similarities and differences of all the beautiful Black folk surrounding me. There is nothing on campus I did not enjoy as a budding freshman. From my roommates in Totty Hall, to food in the cafe, pretty Wednesdays, parties in the circle, as well as parties I probably should not have attended, homecoming, the student union, the Honors College, and an extensive list of places, people and festivities, I loved SU. Like many students at HBCUs across the nation, I was not a fan of the financial aid line or process. Even with that experience, I gained valuable lessons I will carry with me for the rest of my life.

In Louisiana, residents believe in a myth that if you obtain your degree from LSU, the likelihood of you advancing in your goals will increase. The issue with this thinking is not that the opposite is true, but more so that attending *any* accredited school with good programs would place one on a path of becoming a doctor. The esteemed Southern University, without a doubt, falls into that category. I was urged to switch schools. If I wanted to become a doctor, I *"needed"* an LSU degree. Please note that these were not and will never be my words. Some Louisianans seem to overlook the reality that there are many doctors who received their bachelor's degree from Southern University and other schools in our great state. Nevertheless, I heeded the advice given to me and enrolled at LSU in the fall of my sophomore year. My dad was against it, but my mom was for it.

I felt like a traitor! My beloved SU gave me everything I needed. I soon learned that the grass is not always greener on the other side. During my experience at LSU, there was a lack of guidance, nurturing, support and love tailored for the woman I was at that time. I went unseen and unheard. As it is today, most people will never know that I briefly attended LSU. It was the first time in my life that I felt like I did not belong. This could be in part to the culture shock in my own backyard or partly due to the much larger undergraduate population. I cannot speak on LSU's graduate or professional programs. However, for undergrad, I could not go to class and my professors would not know, nor would they care. The class sizes were too large, and they were too busy. I spoke to an academic counselor of whom I have grown fond. In so many words, she encouraged me to do what was best for me.

I transferred back to Southern University and continued to grow academically. Don't get me wrong. LSU is a great school. In addition to life's problems during that period, its undergraduate science/ predental program was just not a fit for what I needed at the time. Southern University treated me like family because I *was* family. I passionately believe that there is a lot of tough love that you get at an HBCU that you will not get at any other school. It resembles what I have received my entire life from aunts, uncles, parents, grandparents and secondary teachers. It is what I am accustomed to. It is how I thrive academically.

I loved Southern University so much that I had to go back and do it again. This time, as a single parent and full-time science teacher, I enrolled in the graduate program at Southern University to obtain my Master of Science in Biology. Same professors, different teaching style. This time around, I had to prove that the nurturing and push from my professors did not go in vain. They were not about to baby me or any of us. There were no excuses in graduate school. My professors worked around my schedule and worked with me at times because they understood I was a full-time teacher. Above all else, they understood I was a full-time parent. They treated us like we were their colleagues, with respect. Graduate school was where

I began to truly apply the lessons taught from my undergraduate experience. Time management was on overload. Being accountable was a must. Everything was earned, not given.

I have had the honor and privilege to be educated by some of the most esteemed and distinguished professors. Because of Southern University's love, support and accomplished faculty, I knew even more that my dream of becoming a doctor could easily be a reality. There were too many people who looked like me, were minorities that were doctors, or taught doctors at some point.

I am currently fourth-year dental student at Howard University College of Dentistry. I have excelled in my studies and held leadership positions in my class and my sorority. My experiences at Southern University were indispensable to the molding that took place within me. SU shaped me into the professional, upstanding, Black woman I am today. With the lessons learned at Southern University, and the covering from my Lord and Savior, there is nothing that any person or school can throw at me that I cannot handle. I can accomplish any goal I set forth. I will be the first Black female dentist from my hometown. There are a multitude of Black and brown professionals hailing from HBCUs across the nation. But O' Southern, dear Southern was the one to pave a path to leading to my career, while showing me that we will always be a people of "firsts" and "manies". I will always represent Southern University because she gave me a second chance. Through my alma mater, I have accomplished many of the goals and dreams I spoke of with such conviction as a little girl. I plan to nurture and give back to the community the way Southern University nurtured and supported me, in true Jaguar fashion.

#WeAreSouthern

About Mieké J. Hampton, M.S.

Mieké Jonelle Hampton is a native of White Castle, Louisiana. She began fertilizing her dreams of becoming a doctor throughout the hallways of White Castle High School with support of her family and teachers. She endeavored to pursue a Baccalaureate degree at the Southern University and A&M College. While at SU, Mieké found a love for mentoring and guiding children. She began her professional experience in the East Baton Rouge Parish School District as a high school science teacher. She continued to expand her teaching repertoire as she returned to her hometown, teaching middle and high school science at her alma mater.

As she molded young children to become future leaders, she decided it was time to shape her own future. She received her Master of Science in Biology in 2016 from Southern University. Mieké continued to shape the minds of her students and mentoring to young girls. During the summer break, she began preparing herself to take the DAT. During this time, she was granted the opportunity to shift gears in the science industry while landing a position as a laboratory technician at ExxonMobil Baton Rouge Polyolefins Plant. She worked there for a year before she transitioned to fulfilling her dream of being a dentist.

Mieké is currently a third-year dental student at Howard University College of Dentistry. At Howard she has maintained exceptional grades while balancing leadership positions, motherhood, and working in the clinic. She is a member of the Alpha Chapter of Delta Phi Sigma Sorority, Incorporated; the *only* interprofessional medical and dental sorority. She has been involved with many community service acts including mentoring young women, performing oral screenings at shelters, participating in food and toiletry drives, and administering the COVID vaccine to the community. She plans to attend a general practice residency upon graduation. Her goal is to open her own practice, educate her patients and the community on preventative oral care measures.

Alicia Renay

The Transition

Alicia Renay

Clear Creek High School Senior Prom. 2008. It was well into the evening. The energy was high, and my classmates and I packed the tiny dancefloor of the transformed local hotel ballroom. The DJ had just begun to fade out Lil Jon & The East Side Boyz "Get Low," one of the most infectious songs of the year. As the music lowered, you could feel the transference in the room. There was an atmospheric shift. I like to call it "the transition." For those of you who grew up in environments where there was no shortage of color, culture or representation, you may be unfamiliar. However, for those of us who grew up in spaces where our own names were a secondary use of identification to being "the Black kid," we know the *transition* all too well.

"The transition" is the moment in the function where it is unwritten, but understood, that everything following will be catered to the majority. With a senior class of 800+ students, the Black population of my high school didn't even make up a single percentage. Not one. There were twelve of us, to be exact. While other backgrounds of color were present, they weren't far ahead in numbers. And just like that, hands still in the air, the DJ had completed his mix, and the next song of the evening had arrived.

With only a few chords to give away the upcoming track, I watched as the majority of my classmates sprinted to the dancefloor. As they rushed in with excitement, "the twelve" quietly exited stage left and headed back to our seats. We watched from the sidelines as they enjoyed a space that had been thoughtfully and carefully curated with them in mind. All together, they screamed out at the top of their lungs the lyrics to *Sweet Home Alabama.*

My entire upbringing came to the forefront in this moment. Recalling the experiences that left me feeling half full and overexposed. From kindergarten, I had been the only (or one of very few) faces of color in my school. I thought about all the times I had been excluded, singled out, made fun of, and adultized. I recalled the genuine anxiety I got every time I changed my hair, *knowing* it would be the topic of conversation the next day. I thought about how many times I found my hair in the hands of strangers, without my consent. I thought about how many post vacation run-ins I had with other students placing their arms next to mine to compare their newly attained shades of tan. How eager kids were to read the word "nigger" out loud during the annual reading of *The Adventures of Huckleberry Finn,* and they were even more eager to look at me while they read it.

I thought about all the conversations my parents had with me on the way to school. I couldn't do what the other kids were doing because I wouldn't be treated the same. I could participate, but not do "too much." I could be present, but not draw any additional attention to myself. I thought about how those conversations inadvertently taught me to conform and assimilate. I was trained to make myself small in order to make others comfortable. I was taught to constantly float between a place of visibility and invisibility—all while I watched my classmates sing at the top of their lungs, without a care in the world. In that very moment, I had had enough. This was about more than song selections at a dance. It was about more than hair or even demographics. This was about a desire to tap into the unused, uncelebrated, and forgotten areas of myself that I had been told to suppress for survival.

Earlier that year, I was introduced to Southern University and A&M College by Mr. Warner, my best friend's dad, who was also a member of the local alumni chapter. As a west coast native, the concept of an HBCU was foreign to me. But I was invited to, and welcomed at, event after event, each encounter pulling me toward something I didn't have words for at the time. Now I know it was the concept of *community.*

I will *never* forget the first time I set foot on the campus of Southern University. I drove over what, at the time, seemed to be a larger-than-life hill, affectionately known as "the hump." Campus was already in mid swing and I had never seen so many people who looked like me in one place. But this was about more than the congregation of Black faces. For me, this was the personification of freedom. For the first time in my life, someone could say "the black girl" and it wouldn't automatically narrow it down to me.

Taking it all in, I observed *everything*. I stopped and watched the interactions, the laughter, the Greeks strolling, the various hairstyles and forms of expression. It appeared as if no one had a care in the world. In this moment, something happened. My shoulders fell. The funny thing is I didn't even realize they had been up prior to this moment. I didn't realize I had lived my entire life on the defense. Unaware of how taxing it was being the only representation of Blackness in my school. Feet always in the blocks, waiting for the sound of the gunshot. For me, this moment was more than an introduction. It was a baptism, and I would be forever changed.

I promised myself I would do everything I set out to do on that campus, even if I had to do it scared to death (and I was). I went on to claim a major of Political Science and I didn't waste any time becoming involved in the university's various organizations. I joined the Student Government Association (SGA), became president of Model U.N., joined a band as the lead vocalist, and became a fall 2011 initiate of the Alpha Tau Chapter of Delta Sigma Theta Sorority, Incorporated.

There are so many memorable and indelible moments I had on the campus of Southern University. However, there is one I will forever cherish. It was the night the election results were announced when Barack Obama was declared the next President of the United States. We spilled out into the streets of campus, celebrating, cheering, crying and reflecting. The energy that was in the air that night, the purity, I have yet to experience again. We celebrated openly and freely. This moment came full circle for me when the Black students from the local predominantly white institution arrived in *droves*. They informed us that, on their campus, the sentiment was much different. In fact, they were burning crosses and hanging Obama's image effigy. Therefore, they decided to come to our campus to celebrate in a safe place, in peace.

That is what my HBCU was to me: *safety*. Safety to express myself how I chose to without being called aggressive or ghetto. Safety to learn about my history from people who looked like me. Safety to mess up without those infractions being charged to my entire race. To be poured into and nurtured by educators who didn't just see me as a number or a statistic. It gave me the tools I needed to enter boardrooms boldly, stand behind my ideas, and demand my worth.

I was born Black, but Southern taught me how to be both Black and proud. And not just proud, but unapologetically so. Not just proud of myself, but to be a part of an institution with such history, such richness. Southern University and A&M College filled holes in me I didn't even know I had. It helped me to discover and nurture who I was. It gave me the freedom to stop accepting who and what the world said I was.

Many people question if HBCUs are still needed and if they are still relevant. The answer is an astounding and overwhelming, "Yes!" I would not be the person I am today if it wasn't for every administrator, professor, staff member and friend that poured into me on that campus. For that, I will *forever* bleed blue and gold.

Now, when I find myself in places where no one looks like me, I no longer shrink and assimilate. I fill rooms. I enter boardrooms and present with grace, intellect, confidence and tenacity. I am often met with gazes of shock, awe and surprise. After which, I am frequently asked, "Where did you go to college again?"

Every time, I lift my head with more pride than the last time and respond, "*Thee* Southern University and Agricultural & Mechanical College."

About Alicia Renay

As a senior trainer in the telecommunications industry, Alicia Davis enjoys traveling the country while acting as a liaison between questions and understanding. With varied interests and an energetic personality, Ms. Davis is an author and editor for her blog sendmeapic.blog, professional singer having have performed for crowds of 50,000+, and "chef" for her friends and family. Alicia also enjoys speech writing and has had the opportunity to use her platform on a national level.

After graduating with her Bachelors in Political Science from thee Southern University and A&M College in 2012, where she served on the SGA senate, President of Model UN, and member of the Alpha Tau chapter of Delta Sigma Theta Sorority Incorporated, she became inspired to help pay it forward and educate those around her about the beauty, relevance, and necessity of the HBCU experience.

When people ask Alicia to describe herself in one word, her answer is always "eclectic."

Alyxandra Bianca Major, MPA

Pride and Excellence
Alyxandra Bianca Major, MPA

Attending an HBCU was the only option for me. I told my high school friends if it wasn't an HBCU, I wasn't filling out a college application to attend their institution. My parents met at an HBCU, Xavier University. Most of my family attended an HBCU also. Most of my life, I attended a school that was truly diverse. I wanted to go somewhere where I could learn about Black history and, for once, not be the minority. I knew if I went to an HBCU, I would be around Black excellence. I knew I would meet Black people from all over the world with different backgrounds and life experiences. Attending an HBCU is an experience like no other. It cannot be duplicated or imitated.

I obtained my bachelor's degree in Criminal Justice in December of 2011 and my master's degree in Public Administration in May of 2016. Like many schools, Southern University and A&M College - Baton Rouge had its share of challenges. From the ridiculously long financial aid lines and technical difficulties with the computer systems, to realizing that all of your classes were dropped and, in order to get them back, you had to walk to each building and request that the chair manually enter you back into your classes, would make any student frustrated beyond measure. These circumstances taught me many life lessons. It taught me how to deal with stressful situations, how to have patience, how to develop emotional intelligence, and the importance of maintaining professionalism.

Many lessons from many professors have stuck with me to this day. In a Geography class, my professor asked us what we were doing for the weekend.

A fellow student said, "I'm taking my girlfriend on a picnic."

I'll never forget the look on our professor's face.

He said, "Young man, do you know where that word comes from?"

"No, sir. I don't."

"Does anyone else know where the word picnic comes from?"

the professor asked the class.

We all looked around at each other, confused. The following class, our professor came with numerous books full of pictures. He informed us that, for this class, we wouldn't discuss geography. Instead, he wanted to have a history lesson about Black history. As he passed the books around, he explained the meaning of what picnic used to mean.

"Pick a nigger," he revealed to us.

My entire class was shaken from the pictures of our ancestors being hung from trees with "explanations" on why they were murdered. They were put on postcards to invite family and friends to join the following week for the next picnic. I don't know about anyone else, but that word now has a stigma for me. I vowed to never say, "I'm going on a picnic" ever again. Instead, I prefer to say, "We are having a cookout at the park or eating crawfish by the lake." This type of professors is what made my HBCU experience memorable. I learned so much about Black history from professors like Dr. Reginald Rackley and the late great Dr. Troy Allen. Dr. Rackley told us when we were in his class to think of it like we were having a seat at the kitchen table for dinner. We were able to have open discussions. I took his class, the African American Experience, the same semester I took Dr. Allen's Black History class. Taking those two classes in one semester enhanced my pro-blackness. Honestly, at times, I went home so angry. I learned so much about what *wasn't* taught to us from kindergarten through the twelfth grade. I didn't understand why anyone would be so hateful and cruel to my ancestors just because of the color of our skin. I took that anger and used it as fuel to educate others. Unless you attend an HBCU, one probably won't experience these types of history lessons. Many do not want us to know. I'm forever grateful for the professors I had at Southern. They didn't shy away from those tough conversations. Instead, they turned them into history lessons.

Homecomings at HBCUs are like big, Black family reunions. The football games are always filled with fans—not only cheering for the football team—but anticipating the sounds from the band during the game and the big show at halftime. The Human Jukebox is the best band in the nation, and this is not up for debate. I appreciate homecoming even more now as an alumnus than I did when I was in undergrad. I get to relive epic moments and spend time with people who I used to see every day to, now, maybe a few times a year. I get to celebrate Black culture without any judgments or explanations.

In my adult life, I am constantly reminded how attending an HBCU helped me become the woman I am today. Many may think otherwise. But my HBCU did prepare me for the real world. I am Black and proud, unapologetically. I work every day in my career to help all individuals in underrepresented groups start and further their careers in healthcare. I formed many lifelong friendships from attending SUBR with people I now consider family. It makes me even more proud that I graduated twice from an HBCU when I see many leaders across the United States who are also HBCU alum. Every day, I am thankful that I attended The Southern University and A&M College. I can proudly say it was one of the smartest decisions I ever made.

About Alyxandra Bianca Major, MPA

Alyxandra Major, MPA is a native of Baton Rouge, Louisiana. She spent secondary school years in Maryland and after graduating high school decided to move back to her hometown and attend The Southern University and A&M College. She has a Bachelor's Degree in Criminal Justice and a Master's Degree in Public Administration (MPA).

Her career in Human Resources began after obtaining her MPA in 2016 while working for the State of Louisiana in Baton Rouge, LA. Currently she works at Ochsner Health which is Louisiana's largest non-profit academic healthcare system where she is the Diversity & Inclusion Career Outreach Specialist. In her position she works with HBCUs, colleges and universities with a large population of diverse students, and community partners to attract and hire top diverse talent. She currently resides in New Orleans, Louisiana.

Andrea Scott

Much More than a Degree
Andrea Scott

Growing up, my parents took me to the Southern University football games at home and away. The excitement, family-friendly environment, the Human Jukebox, the Dolls, the Minidome, homecoming, the games, the blue and gold pride was all contagious. The Bluff is home to a community, my community, being brought together with at least one thing in common: our beloved Southern University Jaguars. College wasn't on my mind in elementary or middle school. But by the time I was in tenth grade, I knew what my next chapter after high school would be. It wasn't until I entered my first class in Stewart Hall on August 16, 2007, that I got my first glimpse into the significance of the journey ahead.

Graduating from Southern University created a footprint in history. During my tenure at SU from August 2007 through May of 2011, I had the privilege of working with some of the greatest minds in my generation. I learned from some of the best instructors I've ever met. By the conclusion of freshman year, I had a friend in just about every area of study on campus, from nursing and biology majors to engineering and business administration. Looking back on it now, that was one of the most vital lessons I learned in undergrad: *networking*! At the time, I thought, *If I make as many friends in as many majors as possible, I'll always have someone to call when I need help with the more challenging courses, such as Biology and Economics.* Almost ten years later, this is a common practice I use when I attend an event, personal or professional.

I chose to major in Political Science because I've always had an interest in policy-making procedures. More specifically, I'm interested in how policies are conceived and how they affect the communities they're designed to assist and/or protect. Each instructor I had offered something of value, something much more than the subject matter of the courses they taught. For example, I met Dr. Revathi Hines during my sophomore year. She was a woman who was small in stature, who had an enormous wealth of knowledge. Somehow, she knew what I needed when I needed it. As time went on, I found myself enrolling in her classes just to be in her class. Passing Dr. Hines' class was no easy task. But I didn't want to just pass. I wanted to excel and earn her respect.

Another one of my most influential instructors was Judge John Michael Guidry. Like Dr. Hines, I met Judge Guidry during sophomore year. He taught American Government. Taking this course was another reason I decided to major in Political Science. He had a teaching style I'd never encountered, but thoroughly enjoyed. He'd lecture the material for two class meetings and use the third meeting for testing prep. At the fourth meeting, Judge Guidry would show up to class with our tests printed on legal-sized paper. On average, the tests were composed of 10-15 questions. On each page, there was one question at the top followed by blank lines for thorough answers. He was tough and knowledgeable about the law and its application to everyday life; yet, he was eager to consider the interpretations from his students.

The faculty and staff are just as much a part of the Jaguar family as the students. They invest their time and energy into every student, inside and outside of the classroom. They exhibited respectable leadership and took a genuine interest in the growth of their students. They, too, have stories and paths that led them to the Bluff. Another professor that comes to mind was a grad student while he was my instructor for a Writing Seminar class. This course was usually for second-semester sophomores. I decided to retake the course to earn a higher grade in a practice called "repeat and delete." We turned in our first writing assignment and the papers were returned to us the following class period. I got a B on the assignment.

At the end of the class period, I walked up to the professor and asked him, "Why didn't I earn an A?"

He looked up and replied to me, "I'm not changing your grade, Scott."

"I'm not asking for a change in my grade. I want to know what my assignment is missing so I know better next time."

He took my paper back and read it again as I sat back down in the front row of the class. Next thing I knew, he was crossing out the

B and changing it to an A. He looked up at me and said, "Honestly, I read so many bad papers, I was frustrated by the time I got to the second half of the stack."

I smiled and said, "Well, the next time you see my name, you'll know to pay closer attention. I don't hand in garbage with my name on it."

About a year or so after I graduated, the same professor asked me to write a letter of recommendation on his behalf for a job in Washington D.C. during the Obama Administration.

At Southern University, I met a host of people from different social backgrounds, ethnic groups and religions. I literally met people from different parts of the world. Some of my instructors were born and raised across the globe. They gave me insight and became a mirror in my life. Our differences and similarities help me navigate through life as an adult with a child of my own. No institution is perfect. However, the highs and lows I experienced on "the yard" taught me how to navigate my path. It gave me overwhelming confidence in my ability to take every low in stride.

Choosing the next chapter upon high school graduation is one of the most important decisions a young adult will make. It is imperative to understand that we can't make it in this world alone. We need to learn from someone else, and then teach others, in order to bridge the gap for generations to come. Southern University is hands down the best decision I made for my career and my life. I stepped onto the campus in pursuit of a degree, but I walked away with so much more.

I walked away with a huge network of family members all over the nation.

About Andrea Scott

Andrea D. Scott, a Baton Rouge, Louisiana native, is a Spring 2011 graduate from Southern University with a Bachelor of Arts in Political Science. She is the proud mother of one son, Andrew Wilson and the daughter of Ardie and Linda Scott III.

Andrea has worked with a multitude of current and former political leaders such as State Senator Regina Barrow, former LA state Senator Yvonne Colomb, and Rep. Pat Smith. Most of her work experience began as a Legislative Aide in the Louisiana House of Representatives and Senate from 2008 until 2016. She is a current and active member of the Parent Union and Economic Justice committees for Step Up Louisiana-Baton Rouge chapter. She has dedicated much of her time and engaging and encouraging her community to stay informed and involved in the political realm.

Andrea has worked in community programs such as the Boys and Girls Club and the Big Buddy program. One of her ultimate goals is to build and maintain a Performing Arts school in the Baton Rouge area where the underprivileged youth can gain access to quality tutoring for all school subjects, hone their skills in music, writing, public speaking, dance, and other art forms.

Edgar Evans, Jr.

Home
Edgar Evans, Jr.

When I think about how far I have come, the memories of Southern University are always deeply embedded in my mind. I can still remember the first time I arrived on campus. There were so many unique senses that I felt then that still feel incredibly real. From the wide view of the Mississippi River from the bluff, the spicy food, and the unique accent from my peers, everything was so new! In a melting pot of African Americans from all over the world, I was exposed to many different cultures within Black culture that I never knew existed. I had truly arrived in a "New World." After my initial homesickness, I settled in and met a group of young men who I am still friends with to this day. I learned from their life perspectives and made it a priority to be the best friend to them as best as I could. This camaraderie was apparent throughout the campus. What we called "cliques" at the time were support systems and the foundations of friendship. I felt this same support throughout the faculty, staff and alumni. Even though I was hundreds of miles away from where I grew up, this was my home. I learned many life lessons during my time at Southern. Without them, I don't know where I would be.

Once I left Southern, I moved to Atlanta, a city that I always wanted to reside in. I arrived during a time of economic downturn and had a naïve view of how easy it would be to find work. I didn't take advantage of the career fairs and connections that Southern provided while I was there. That was one of the biggest mistakes I made as a young man. After selling everything I owned, I lived briefly in a Motel 6 off of Lawrenceville Highway in Atlanta. I stayed there for about a month as I needed proof of employment to sign a lease for an apartment. My first job in Atlanta was a part-time position at Best Buy, selling televisions. I realized that I had just spent years and thousands of dollars for an education that I couldn't use for my benefit. I only had myself to blame. I didn't join any clubs or do any internships during school. I didn't have any mentors or a plan once I left school. I was so immersed in the culture of partying and hanging out that I totally lost sight of the real world. I had every opportunity at my fingertips, but I didn't take advantage of it. Over the next year, I worked multiple part-time jobs as I fell further into debt.

After I received an eviction notice from my apartment building, I sat and thought to myself, *There has to be more.* At the time, I had a good friend who also went to Southern that was going back to Baton Rouge for a couple of days to hang out. After offering me to go with him, I gladly caught a ride and headed to my old home. My first order of business was to talk to the dean of the college of business. I unexpectedly waited outside of his office for a meeting. Once I was able to see him, I told him my story and about the strong need for a salaried position. It just so happened that there was a career fair the following day. He told me if I came, he would help me find a salaried position. After our talk, I realized that our twenty-minute meeting had taken a year too long to have. The next day, I used a suit that was provided by an old classmate and attended the career fair. While there, I met with many companies. But I really hit it off with Sherwin Williams Paints. After three interviews, I was offered the position of Assistant Manager in a small town called Opelousas, Louisiana.

I was finally making a good living. I got a chance to get out of the hole I'd dug myself into and had time to reflect. I realized that I had wasted so much time. I started to think about all that I had been through and, more importantly, where I was going. I originally came to Southern with the help of a golf scholarship. Golf was my first love, and I had once dedicated my life to playing professionally full-time. I found out quickly after college that one needed the time and resources to do so. On a hot, summer day after working alone in the paint store for many hours, I decided that I would do everything in my power to reach my childhood dream. As I reflected over the past ten years or so, I knew that making this happen would all be on me. That realization, coupled with the struggles that I had post-college, motivated me like never before. After I saved up for another couple of months, I took a golf job, making minimum wage at Atlanta Country Club. If I could work at a golf course, it would give me a free place to practice and work on my game. My short-term goal was to be an instructor at a private golf club. Then, I would be able to branch out and do my own thing.

But to do so, I had to get a year of private club experience. When I met with the head golf professional at the club, I told him of my desire to teach golf at a private club. He told me that if I worked hard, he would use all of his resources to help me. As soon as I heard that, I knew I was in the right place. Again, years after college, I was making minimum wage. But this time, it was different. I had experience, but more importantly, I had an unmatched work ethic and hunger. After working at the country club for three months, I was promoted to assistant caddy master. I also received tips when I cleaned people's golf clubs. I started making more money than I did with Sherwin Williams. I also developed relationships with the membership that was affluent and held top business positions in major Atlanta companies. Four months following my initial promotion, one of the assistant golf professionals got out of the business. I went to speak with the head golf professional and told him that I would like to be considered for the position. He agreed to give me an interview. A couple of weeks later, I was promoted to assistant golf professional. I was the first African American to ever be a part of the professional staff in the club's 57-year history.

Since being promoted, my life has changed. I have since become the director of golf instruction at the club (a position that I created and pitched myself). I have written and released a golf instructional book entitled, *Flawless*, and I currently host/produce a local Atlanta golf television show entitled *Saturday Foursome* that airs on NBC Atlanta. I have other entrepreneurial projects that I am working on that will make me a millionaire by 2022. My life changed when I decided that I wanted more and would work hard to achieve my dreams. My life also changed when I went to Southern. Southern helped me when I was at my lowest point. As I look back now, it has given me so much that I use in my day-to-day life. I will forever be indebted to Southern. I have no doubt that no one will be able to give back more than I will one day. It's the faith and hard work that makes your reality happen. When you figure that out, you realize anything is possible. I am still chasing that childhood dream, and I can't wait to bring my victories back home to Southern.

Edgar Evans, Jr. is a self-published author, golf professional, television host/producer and entrepreneur. He currently resides in Atlanta.

About Edgar Evans, Jr.

Edgar Evans Jr. is a golf professional and author originally from Augusta, GA. He began playing the game at 11 years old when his father purchased a set of golf clubs at a yard sale. Even though Edgar Sr. didn't play golf, he wanted to find a sport that his son could excel at. After getting hit by the golf bug, Edgar Jr. taught himself how to play the game through reading books and watching The Golf Channel. Through hard work and dedication Edgar made his high school golf team and parlayed his good play into receiving a golf scholarship at Southern University in Baton Rouge, Louisiana. After college Edgar worked multiple jobs trying to stay afloat, but realized that he wasn't living his dream. After a coming to God moment he realized that his life's calling was going to be in the game of golf.

He left a well paying managerial job at Sherwin Williams to go get private club golf experience at Atlanta Country Club. His hope was that if he got a year of experience at a private club that he would then be qualified to work on a professional staff at a good club in the Atlanta area. The position that he took at A.C.C was for the cart staff and the pay was minimum wage. After a summer of hard work Edgar was promoted to assistant caddy master. He continued with his intense work ethic, and after a couple more months he asked to be considered for an assistant golf professional position that was opening up at the club. After the interview process, Edgar was offered the position as an assistant golf professional.

Since being promoted he has been able to play in professional golf tournaments, become the head instructor at the club, and has authored his first golf instructional book entitled, "Flawless." Edgar used the proceeds from his book sales to fund shooting the pilot, "Saturday Foursome." His television program is set to stream on Amazon Prime beginning in the fall of 2021. His future plans are to write more books, produce golf television content, and play professional golf.

Dr. Shanna R. Warner

Southern: A Family Tradition
Dr. Shanna R. Warner

"O Southern, dear Southern.!"

For as long as I can remember, I have loved Southern University. I fell in love with Southern, and began to bleed blue and gold, at an early age. My family, The Oree Warner family, has had a strong presence on the campus since the 1960s. Seven out of eleven of my paternal grandparents' children, including my dad, graduated from Southern. When my youngest aunt graduated, my grandparents were acknowledged. In addition, my parents met, fell in love and graduated from Southern. Three out of four of their kids and a granddaughter graduated from there. I can't even begin to count the number of cousins who also have graduated from Southern.

I remember going to alumni conferences over the summer with family as a child. One of the best ones was in Orlando. I went to Disney World with Southern's marching band, The Human Jukebox, and Miss Southern. You couldn't tell me that I didn't have the best "what did you do over the summer" story when I returned to school in the fall. During football season, we spent most Saturday nights in A. W. Mumford Stadium or traveling with the Jaguar Nation. As I got older, I chose to be there over many of my major high school events. A fond memory and family tradition was celebrating Thanksgiving together in Bogalusa. Then, we all went to New Orleans for the Bayou Classic.

The traditions and legacy established by my family made it easy to make Southern my school of choice. It also helped that I was selected and awarded a scholarship to be a part of the Dolores Margaret Richard Spikes Honors College. When I arrived on the bluff in the fall of 1999, I knew I was exactly where I was supposed to be. Being in the honors college really helped me become a better student. I was surrounded by students from across the world who were extremely smart, focused and determined. Our dean, Dr. Beverly Dixon Wade, really empowered and cultivated us. She was a force to be reckoned with. She did not mince words and she did not believe in cutting corners. She always demanded the best from all of her students.

As a member of the honors college, students were required to take honors courses. Because I was a biology major, I was required to take honors biology. Professor Florence Robinson, who was extremely passionate about science, was my teacher. Her class helped me become more disciplined as a student. It taught me to fight for what I believed in. In addition to teaching, she was an environmental activist who took on big chemical plants that brought toxins into her neighborhood and on our campus. Dr. Brian Lewis was also one of my teachers in the biology department. He did not do anything average. He wanted us to be exceptional. One of his favorite sayings was, "Ignorance ought to keep you up at night." Whenever we were not giving our best, he would let us know. College was an adjustment. I was away from home and had to learn to be disciplined amongst lots of distractions. So many professors helped push me along the way. Mrs. Wellons, Dr. Spencer, Dr. Comminey, Ms. James and so many others poured into my life. They gave me the knowledge and confidence to succeed.

Living on campus in Washington Hall made it easy to make friends. It was one of the honors dormitories. So, more than likely, I had several honors classes with those who lived in the dorm. It was like a big family. We held each other accountable, studied together, decorated for games and went to the cafeteria together. One of the ultimate betrayals was going to the cafeteria without asking your friends if they wanted to go. I also made friends via Student Government Association, through other classes and through other organizations.

It was through student government and other organizations, specifically Alpha Kappa Alpha Sorority, Incorporated, Beta Psi chapter, that I found friends to establish a work/life balance. We studied, partied, tailgated, went to football games and even did community service together. We had a blast going to Club Upscale, Poets and Night Life. I went to so many Alpha, Kappa and Omega parties. If we really wanted to be fancy, we went to Perfect 10 parties. Homecoming and Springfest were always live. Cash Money Records really did take over for the '99 and 2000. My freshman year, they shut the homecoming concert all the way down.

Sophomore year, UGK performing at the homecoming concert was a close second. We went to all home games and got on the spirit bus for any away game we could. The best away game was at FAMU in 2001. After we successfully beat their football team, our students rushed the field as if we had won the Super Bowl. They had to turn the sprinklers on to get us off the field. Tailgating on campus was an all-day thing. Alumni and friends really laid on Southern hospitality. We could literally walk out by the RVs and some of the older fans would volunteer to feed us. On rare occasion, if no one did, the Omegas or the Alphas always had food to offer.

I am profoundly grateful for Southern University. It has given me lifelong friends who have become family. It provided me with an education from some of the best professors. And it was pivotal in helping me become a successful dentist. I learned better study habits. I learned to problem solve, and I was given a solid foundation in basic sciences.

When I went to dental school at Meharry, I felt the love of the Jaguar Nation. Several of my professors, and a few classmates, had gone to Southern. On the first day of class, one of my professors, Dr. Moses, told me that he and another doctor had come to Southern in the 1970s to help perform autopsies on two students. Denver Smith and Leonard Brown were peacefully protesting with thousands of other students at the administration building when they were killed by law enforcement. Law enforcement claimed that they were shot in self- defense. But the autopsies determined that both Smith and Brown had been shot from behind.

Because it has given so much to me, I am forever indebted to Southern. I am an active, life member of the Southern University Alumni Federation. I am one of the youngest founding members of the Southern University System Foundation's 1880 Society. I believe it is imperative that I continue to support my institution to ensure perpetuity for generations to come. The fight song rings in my ear.

"Southern University, defenders of the gold and blue! We will always be loyal and raise a cheer for you."

About Dr. Shanna R. Warner

Dr. Shanna R. Warner is a native of Bogalusa, Louisiana. In the Spring of 2003, she received her Bachelor of Science in Biology from Southern University and A&M College and Doctor of Dental Surgery degree (DDS) from Meharry Medical College in 2009. After Dental School, she returned to Baton Rouge, LA where she is currently a General Dentist at a Federally Qualified Health Center. She is also a Dentist Reviewer and Consultant for a national independent medical examiner company.

Dr. Warner is deeply involved in her community, performing countless hours of service year in and year out. She has volunteered with the Louisiana Dental Association's Mission of Mercy to provide free dental care in the Greater Baton Rouge region and volunteered with the city of Baton Rouge for free dental clinic. She has also volunteered with Team Smile in partnership with the New Orleans Saints to provide free dental care to children in the greater New Orleans area. In addition, she has done countless screenings, including Give Kids A Smile Day and has participated in many health fairs and career days.

Dr. Warner is involved in various professional and community organizations including the American Dental Association, Louisiana Dental Association, Greater Baton Rouge Dental Association, National Dental Association, and Capital City Dental Association. She is a member of Louisiana Oral Health Coalition and Alpha Kappa Alpha Sorority, Incorporated - Gamma Eta Omega chapter. She also serves on the board of directors for the Louisiana Youth Seminar and Ivy Foundation.

Dr. Warner strives to continue to advance the legacies of Southern University and Meharry Medical College. She is a Life member of the Southern University Alumni Federation where she served as the co-chair for the Southern University Young Alumni Network (SUYAN) and served on the 2016 and 2018 Nominations and Elections committee. She is a member of the Southern University Alumni-Home Chapter. Shanna is also a founding member of the Southern University 1880 Society where she is a board member and

---

currently serves as Secretary. She is also a proud donor and an active member of the Meharry Medical College Alumni Association.

Dr. Warner lives by the words of Luke 12:48: "To whom much is given, much is expected." She believes that these words convict her and strengthen her love and support for the institutions and organizations that have molded her over the years. One of her greatest joys is mentoring students. Whether it is providing guidance to those interested in pursuing a career in dentistry, allowing students to shadow her in her office, or connecting students with other healthcare professionals, Dr. Warner will do what she can to help students succeed. Her accomplishments, compassion, and authenticity are fruits of the seeds that were sown into her not only during her time at Southern University and Meharry, but by the people around her who themselves were products of the same institutions who blazed the trail that she follows today.

Fallon R. Hamilton, Esq.

That Sea of Black Faces
Fallon R. Hamilton, Esq.

Lost in a sea of Black faces...
No awkward feelings,
Nor uncomfortable spaces.
All is well.
Everyone is good.
There is no competition in the neighborhood.
Black people dancing with faces full of joy.
Thriving and shining is every girl and every boy.
Here there is no sorrow,
Only promises of prosperity land.
Simply happy Black people,
Untouched by alabaster hands.

I first stepped foot on the campus of Southern University and A&M College almost exactly twenty-one years ago. I found myself intimidated by the hundreds, rather thousands, of people who surrounded me as I stood in the middle of the "Mini-Dome" trying to appear cool while I clung to my mother's side as we completed the registration process. Although I grew up on the northwest side of Houston, Texas in the historically Black community known as Acres Homes, in that moment, my first thought was that I had never seen so many Black people in one place at the same time! Looking back, it almost sounds foolish that my then eighteen-year-old self felt so amazed to be that deeply submerged into a space where people the same hue as I ebbed and flowed in every direction. I had never seen Black people walk with so much confidence and sense of belonging before in my entire life. I saw Black people of every shade, with glorious crowns of hair adorning their heads, as if they were royalty. I saw regal Black men wearing bright colors with pride so vibrant that I had to do several double takes. I briefly remember my mother saying to me with a sense of knowing she was sure I had never seen this many Black people before. She was right. I had not. I did not possess the level of comfort and security that was on display that day. I was genuinely afraid that I would become lost in that sea of Black faces.

My freshman year of college, I resided in Washington Hall, in what was affectionately known as "The Front" where members of the Southern University Honors College were housed. As we begrudgingly moved all my belongings into my room, the realization that my family would be leaving me there alone sunk in. I tried to remain calm and project a confident demeanor. But inside, I was truly terrified. As parents cleared out, it was evident that a lot of the students who lived nearby were going home to be with their families for the extended weekend before classes started. By nightfall, as I peered out my door, I realized that the hallway had become deserted. Not only was I alone in my room, but the entire hallway also appeared to be empty. I remember clinging to a teddy bear I had brought to campus with me. I blasted my music to silence the loneliness that had started to take over me. As the night progressed, I heard footsteps nearing. I was greeted by several then strangers who had heard my music blaring in the hallway and recognized the artists. Fortunately, I had been listening to local Houston artists. The visitors who were familiar with the tune were also from Texas. Instantly, a bond was made, and I no longer felt that overwhelming sense of loneliness. Natural connections like that became commonplace on campus.

By the end of that first semester, I found myself with a new, heightened sense of awareness and my Blackness. I met people from Haiti, from all parts of the United States, and from the continent of Africa. They were Black like me, young and determined to leave Southern University better than they had arrived. They were proud of the culture, and they instilled that same pride in me. I was hungry for knowledge. I met as many people as I could, and I experienced as many things as I could. I wanted to know where the accents in southern Louisiana derived from, and why there were such a stark difference than the dialect I was used to in my family hometown of Mansfield in northern Louisiana. I read books from authors I had never been exposed to, discovering James Baldwin and other artists from the Harlem Renaissance. I watched other students share pieces of art they created and poems they had written during spoken word nights in The Union. I read strongly worded think pieces in The Southern Digest where student reporters discussed the current events in the world with such fervor and precision that I thought I was reading excerpts from *The New York Times*. By the time I went home, I had been told I was beautiful in over a dozen dialects. I walked with a newfound sense of confidence that I never felt at home. By that second week of Christmas break, I knew I had to get back home to Baton Rouge!

I never anticipated myself changing so much in only a few months. But the transformation was profoundly noticeable in not only myself, but the people I had returned home to for the break in Houston. My friends immediately commented on the way I appeared to radiate confidence. I was no longer the shy girl who was more comfortable blending into the crowd than standing on the forefront of it. I walked with pride. I walked as if I belonged in every space I occupied. I did not shy away from the spotlight. After all that time, the girl who had always been more comfortable with only interacting with a few people had finally found her voice. I discovered a strength that I did not know I possessed. I had something to say, and I finally had the courage to speak boldly and unapologetically when I said it.

Before that first year of my collegiate career ended, I had interviewed and was extended an invitation to be a staff reporter for *The Southern Digest*. I had written and performed several pieces of my original poetry in front of other students. I no longer felt lost in the crowd. I went on to share my voice throughout the tenure of my college career, writing for the newspaper. I challenged myself to try even more things. I participated in pageants and fashion shows. I took a semester off for an externship with the Louisiana Legislative Black Caucus/Louisiana Legislative Women's Caucus, which then led to my desire to pursue a career in law.

Southern University was the catalyst that changed the trajectory of my life. Feeling lost in that sea of Black faces ultimately helped me discover so much of myself and who I was destined to become. The connections and knowledge I received, and the unique ways I found my voice, have taken me far in my legal career. Spanning over one decade, I have had the opportunity to advocate for the rights of many others who may have felt lost in a crowd. In 2018, I went back to my love of poetry that was ignited in the Smith-Brown Memorial Union at Southern University. I published my first collection of poetry, which went on to become a number one bestseller on Amazon. I have also shared my voice in several anthologies.

The opportunities at my beloved institution were without limits. My love of Southern University is embedded deep within my soul. Southern blessed me with so many great things. Most recently, Southern awarded me my greatest accomplishments to date, being recognized as a Southern University Alumni Federation Forty Under 40 Award recipient. I am thankful for my institution. I am forever grateful to that sea of Black faces that welcomed me as one of their own.

Southern University, I thank you!

About Fallon R. Hamilton, Esq.

Fallon Renee Hamilton graduated from Southern University in December of 2004, earning a Bachelor of Arts degree in Political Science with honors. While at Southern, she was a staff writer for the award-winning Southern Digest and a member of the Southern University Honors College. Her journey post-Southern led her back home to Houston, Texas, where she enrolled in and graduated from Texas Southern University- Thurgood Marshall School of Law in May 2008. She has been a licensed attorney for over ten years and currently works as an Attorney at Lone Star Legal Aid, which is the 4th largest provider of free civil legal services in the country. Her dedication to public service has allowed her to serve on the Board of Directors for several non-profit organizations and participate in numerous community service endeavors serving those in Houston and the surrounding areas.

Always an avid reader and writer, Fallon used books as her outlet both creatively and as a form of self-care. In 2018, her first book entitled "An Ode" was published and debuted as a number one best- seller in African American Poetry on Amazon. In the Summer of 2019, Fallon co-authored her second book entitled "Super Woman Survival Stories" which also debuted as a best-seller on Amazon. In 2020, during the height of the pandemic, Fallon co-founded an organization called A Tribe Called Manifest to provide self-care, wellness, and an appreciation for the power of manifestation to Black and Brown people. She facilitates intention writing workshops, and full moon collectives, as she assists others with manifesting the lives they deserve. Fallon enjoys sharing her love of story-telling and poetry writing with the world and is currently working on her debut fiction novel.

Keithan Oubre

How Southern University Shaped Who I Am
Keithan Oubre

For many people, college is where they find themselves. Others feel college builds on a preexisting foundation. For myself, Southern changed the way I thought and approached everything in life. It began the moment I stepped on campus.

Before attending Southern, I enrolled at several schools, earning an associate degree in Instrumentation. I also attended another university in the south Louisiana region. It was at Southern, though, that I learned the importance of networking and being the best representation of my university.

My first collegiate experience at a predominantly white institution felt as if I was in a maze. I wasn't sure where to go or where to start. Coming from a small country town, I was truly a minority. My required courses were no longer available at times that worked to my advantage. I was too late in the registration process because I was indecisive. It definitely was a hard lesson learned. My goal was to pick a direction and run as hard as I could toward it.

Years later, my enrollment at Southern is when it all came into place. My friends and their circles grew. Some worked for the university. Others were from a family lineage of Southern board members. I registered as soon as I could. While waiting in an office, I ran into a friend from my hometown of Vacherie, Louisiana. He worked in recruiting for the university and asked if I needed assistance. Of course, I took him up on the offer. At that moment, my education on life during and after college began. I was introduced to so many employees and numerous counselors, which gave me the head start I'd never had before. It was not only him that helped, but friends I connected with prior to my first day.

One of my first professors taught me the importance of not only networking, but also maintaining those connections. Don't just appear when you have a need. If passing by their office or building, stop by, even if it's only for a few minutes. Something as small as that is the difference between being greeted by name and, "What's your name again?" By doing this, I've eliminated the third party. Now you have a personal relationship. One morning, I received an early morning phone call from the dean. I met him earlier that week and gave him my phone number. He asked if I had completed the registration for the upcoming semester. I wasn't finished at the moment, but I was instructed to meet him within an hour. Less than an hour after our discussion, my registration was complete.

After graduating and transitioning into my professional career, this is when I utilized my experience and the importance of being the first impression of being a Southern graduate for most of my new coworkers. They only knew of Southern from what was reported by local news. The narrative of my school was told from the view of a person on the outside looking in on the news. It was negative and flat out wrong. I took on the challenge of changing not only their view, but others they would encounter. If I could change their perspective of Southern University, I would open the door to opportunity to those coming behind me.

In my first corporate position working at a CPA firm, I came in with an open mind and reminded myself of the marathon, not the sprint. Work hard now and enjoy the fruit of the seeds I sowed. In the process, I was recognized by partners of the firm for my work and consistency. In doing so, I was promoted to the Fraud Waste and Abuse department. My supervisors were former FBI directors. I never dreamt that after walking on stage to receive my bachelor's degree, I would have a seat at a table of such. I took it all in stride. I was grateful. At this point, I was assigned the reasonability of assisting and training new hires. I exceeded my initial goal. From working within a team of ten to fifteen individuals, my reach was that of 150 to 200+ individuals. I still have the relationships I built then. I can call anyone whom I had the pleasure of working with and hear the excitement in their voice. When I visit home, I make time for not just my family, but as many of them as I can.

My affirmation materialized when a former classmate was interviewed by a manager who I worked closely with on several projects. The manager asked the applicant if she knew me and spoke about her interactions with me. She replied, "Yes! We had a few classes together and worked on a few projects. I was quiet. But once we got past the ice breaker stage, my willingness to help was evident. Management told me before meeting her that those were the first questions that came to mind. They wanted to know if she knew me and how much we interacted. After my former coworker replied, they decided to hire her. Both said the interview process may have been five minutes, at most. My personal goal was achieved and surpassed. When they heard of Southern University, I was the first person that came to mind. Due to my impression on them, the view on Southern was one of truth. It was no longer based on the opinion of another. Upon revisiting the college of business, I thank my professors for the valuable advice. I didn't work twice as hard for my own gain. I did so for those coming behind me. I want to give them opportunities I did not have. Just as my friends and those I know opened doors for me at Southern, I opened doors for those I didn't know.

I continued to work toward this personal goal in every aspect of my life, in the workplace and in general. You never know who you may run into just from grabbing a cup of coffee. I'm grateful and thankful for all those I've encountered in my journey and look forward to those I will encounter.

About Keithan Oubre

Keithan Oubre is a Senior Accountant at Baylor College of Medicine in Houston, Texas. He is responsible for reconciling several funds and grants which aid pediatric cancer research. He graduated from Southern University and A&M College with bachelor's degrees in Business Management (2009) and Accounting (2012).

After graduating he lived in New Orleans, Louisiana for five years before moving to Houston. He is currently working towards obtaining a CPA license. Before working at Baylor College of Medicine, he was a Forensic Accountant at Postlewaite and Netterville CPA firm.

Langston A. Williams

Jag Wars
Langston A. Williams

The year was 2007. I was a young, naïve college kid embarking on a new experience. I didn't know what to expect. As the outgoing guy I was, I was always seeking to create waves and make changes. I decided to start first with where I lived: Bradford Hall, the male honors dorm. I decided it would be smart to run for an office at my dormitory to make my mark. Little did I know that this position was one practically in title only. The president of a dorm had pretty much no authority to make any changes. Those who know me know I don't just *do* things. I *overdo* them. Not only did I run for president of the dorm, but I also ran for vice president of the dorm. I was determined to get in there.

I'm sure I drew much ire from my opponents for my decision to run for more than one position. Then, elections came. I campaigned heavily for these positions that meant practically nothing, but I do everything at 110%. I'm actually not sure that anyone else campaigned. When the results came, I had won both president and the vice president. I ended up relinquishing the vice president position to my opponent. I wasted no time scheduling multiple meetings a week.

For the first meeting, my cabinet members were shambled and dressed in sweats. I, on the other hand, came dressed in a suit and tie. No one could tell me anything. As I rolled out my agenda for accomplishing my extremely ambitious platform, my cabinet members only halfway listened to me. Some took notes. Some played on their phones. All were just waiting on me to stop running my mouth so that they could leave. When I finally stopped talking, and called the meeting to an end, one of them asked what would become one of the most important questions anyone could ask someone else at Southern University: "You hit the cafe yet?" We all walked over to Mayberry Dining Hall after the meeting and rounded out this bonding experience with a meal that may have seemed subpar to some. But at the beginning of my college career, no one could've told me that it wasn't a five-star dining experience.

Again, being the overly ambitious president of the dorm that I was, I couldn't just have one meeting a week. I had to have three and four meetings a week. My cabinet members were called together many more times that week to further work toward my agenda for change and progress at Bradford Hall. While at first, I think I was likely just the annoying guy who took a title-only position way too seriously, it seemed as if we soon warmed up to each other. Boring cabinet meetings soon turned into boisterous, jovial gatherings. At some point, I wasn't sure if I was still calling cabinet meetings because I believed in the agenda or because I just enjoyed the companionship and company. What else was I going to do as a freshman with way too much free time before getting hungry every day?

Then, Jag Wars was announced. A series of games, scavenger hunts and quests where teams of five all competed for glory, bragging rights and the ultimate prize: tickets to the Bayou Classic. The first of the events was dodgeball. The vice president saw the advertisement and suggested we sign up. Being the spry, young freshmen in peak physical condition, we felt we were a shoo-in for the gold. We signed up. We could've probably called ourselves The Bradford Cabinet, but it wasn't cool enough. Temporarily, we put down the name "TBA" until we could figure out something better. We did some extremely basic workouts in preparation for the big dodgeball game to ensure victory during what would've been our normal meeting times. Other times, we got together to brainstorm a team name. We never could come up with anything we all agreed upon.

Finally, the big day came. We were only slightly more in shape, mentally exhausted from trying to think of a team name. We were filled with way too much anxiety for the night to actually go in our favor. As we approached the check-in table, we were asked if we ever thought of a team name. We rattled off a few last second ideas for a team name, all to everyone else's disapproval. The person checking in got annoyed at us holding up the line and finally said, "Okay, so Team TBA." We looked at each other and answered, "Okay. That works." This name stuck for years to come.

As TBA took the court in the first round of the dodgeball tournament, we had a new level of confidence. No one could tell us that we couldn't win. So, imagine our surprise when our team was surgically picked apart in a matter of mere seconds as the referee blew the whistle. The vice president, the team captain, was quickly picked off. The secretary and I were not long after. The Sergeant-at-Arms threw a ball that went horribly off course. It hit one of the judges, leading to him getting put out. It was pretty terrible. The vice president took it extremely hard. We'd trained all week for this moment. We were physically superior to our competition ... in his mind, at least. Yet, we could not last the full game. We stayed to watch the rest of the tournament, then made our walk of shame to the cafeteria.

After the Jag Wars disappointment, I don't even think I was still calling meetings. But, out of habit, we all met up in the lounge of the dorm. I think we finally moved past the point of just being dorm political associates and teammates to being friends when we decided to move the meetings from the lounge to my dorm room. After all, my roommate was never in the room. Jag Wars was definitely a bonding experience that I underestimated the power of. Going through something together can cause a relationship to blossom with those also going through it with you. We definitely experienced this phenomenon first semester freshman year.

Fortunately, Jag Wars was not a one-time thing. They brought it back two more times in the fall of 2010 and 2011. When it did, we reassembled the squad and prepared again. However, the next two times, we took home the gold! Those were actually two of my most epic Bayou Classic experiences to date because we felt we fought and *earned* those tickets. We were also surrounded by good company when we actually got there. To this day, the cabinet and I, who I from here on will refer to as TBA, have remained close friends. Not many days pass without talking to them, and we have probably the most popping group chat that's ever existed. Lord, don't ever let there be another iCloud hack and leak.

It was at Southern University where I met and made lifelong friends. It was at Bradford Hall where we grew close. It was at Jag

Wars where we solidified our friendship. Honestly, had I not gone to an HBCU, I question if I would have had the same kind of friends or if I'd even have friends at all? Attending an HBCU was integral to me finding my tribe. Not everyone in life does. If you're considering a college to attend, maybe you should try your luck, too. I would try Southern University.

Highly recommend.

Five stars.

About Langston A. Williams

Langston A. Williams is a 2012 third generation graduate of Southern University and A&M College. Originally from Gulfport, Mississippi, he is now a filmmaker in New Orleans. Having completed a dual degree in Mass Communications and Theatre Arts, he went on to pursue and earn his Masters in Film Production at the University of New Orleans.

Langston Williams has worked on a plethora of films and television series in New Orleans, Boston, and Cleveland including films like Queen and Slim, Antebellum, and The Highwaymen, and shows like Queen Sugar, The Purge, and NCIS: New Orleans. Outside of larger studio films, Langston has been directing short films, music videos, and supporting his own latest film Stay Woke in the film festival circuit where it was accepted into 45 festivals including the world›s biggest and most prestigious film festival, the Cannes Film Festival, and has won at 23 festivals.

While at Southern University, Langston was involved in a number of campus organizations and was very active on campus. He became a member of the Alpha Eta Chapter of Iota Phi Theta Fraternity Inc. in Fall 2009. In his time at Southern he served in the Student Government Association as a Sophomore Class Senator, the SGA Vice President, and a Senior Class Justice. He was active in the schools theatre club The Lacumba Players, and participated in a number of stage plays both on stage and backstage. Along with cohosts Adam Powell and Jeremy Jason, Langston hosted the first web radio show at Southern University's The Bluff Web Radio station. In spring of 2008, Langston had the highest GPA in the University College before transferring over to the schools Honors College. Also in 2008, he worked as a Resident Assistant in Boley Hall. When pageant seasons rolled around, Langston won crowns in the Mr. Freshman pageant in 2007, the Mr. Collegiate 100 Pageant in 2008, the Mr. Blue and White Pageant in 2011, and the Mr. AWS (Association for Women's Students) Pageant in 2011.

Marissa Jones

Delayed, But Not Denied
Marissa Jones

"O Southern, dear Southern, we owe our all to thee!" No truer words could be spoken from a small-town girl from Crystal Springs, Mississippi, who made an unpopular decision to attend a school that she didn't know much about. It was an unpopular decision that turned into one of the best decisions of her life. Born and raised on the campus of Jackson State University, with the intention of sending ACT scores to the University of Southern Mississippi, it was by accident (or more likely destiny) that she sent them to Southern University. That move alone resulted in a fall open house invitation that brought her to the campus of Southern University and Agricultural and Mechanical College for the first time. This changed her life forever.

Before I could cross "the hump", I knew this was the place for me. The people, the atmosphere, the Columbia blue and gold. The campus was full of trees and open grass where I could sit with friends or read books, like the scenes I had seen on "A Different World". That day, I got a glimpse of what was destined to change my life: The Southern University Marching Band, affectionately known as The Human Jukebox. After one song, that was it. I was going to Southern University, and I was going to be a part of that band. It was that performance, that day, that confirmed my heart now belonged on Scott's Bluff.

A little over a year from my first introduction to Southern, I was accepted. I proudly walked into the office of Dr. Isaac Greggs for my audition for The Human Jukebox. I had heard the whispers of little to no females being allowed in this band. If by chance I did make it in, there were things, like not walking on the grass, or not perming my hair until the Bayou Classic, that I might encounter. None of that meant anything to me. I was going to be in this band. To my dismay, when I walked in, Dr. Greggs proudly told me that he was full for my instrument. He told me to try again next year. I didn't have an opportunity to play one scale to try to change his mind. Boy, was I upset. But that truly lit a fire in me! I may have been delayed, but I would not be denied.

With my mom upset and demanding I return home, where I had full academic and band scholarships waiting on me, I politely told her it was okay. I was going to Southern University. I went on to enjoy everything about my first semester at Southern. I learned how to eat crawfish and how to jig. I learned Louisiana slang and culture, and so many more things I had never experienced, even though I was born and raised only an hour and forty-five minutes away. Still, I never lost sight of the goal at hand. In the spring semester, I joined the symphonic band, where I shed and sharpened my skills. So, when it was time for auditions again, they would have no choice but to choose me!

With Mr. Lawrence Jackson as the new Director of Bands, I was granted the opportunity not only to become a member of the Southern University Marching Band, but to also be a part of what I now know was history in the making! When I walked in the band hall with 100+ people I had never seen before, I looked around and something was distinctly different. There were way more young women present than I had seen the year before. Little did I know, I was joining the largest group of female crabs that had ever appeared in The Human Jukebox. What a difficult journey we had, but I would not trade it for anything in the world. That experience is something that has shaped me into the person I am today. Adversity had been met before my freshman year by not being allowed to audition, but now I had arrived! I made it, but there were a lot of people who were not excited to see me, nor my crab sisters, in that uniform we all had longed to wear.

By the end of the first day, I made a promise to myself that nothing would stand in the way of me finishing the course. Every day, I would give my all! Throughout my marching band career, I received many accolades, including Entertainer of the Year and Highest Academic Average. I was fortunate to complete all four years, which allowed me to receive the greatest reward of all: our version of a letterman's jacket, which we call a "wool". Receiving that jacket is a supreme achievement because many start the journey, but few make it all the way through. Outside of the marching band,

I had to "get my lesson" as Mr. J would say. I excelled in my major of Therapeutic Recreation and Leisure Studies, maintaining a 4.0 for the majority of my collegiate career. I graduated Magna Cum Laude in four years.

In addition to Southern, The Human Jukebox gave so much to me. In 2012, when I learned of an opportunity to formally give back to the program, I jumped at the chance! The Human Jukebox Alumni Association (HJAA) evolved under the leadership of Jefferson Reese, Jr. and a group of band alumni. It was my esteemed pleasure to become a member of the Board of Trustees. Through this organization, I was able to be an integral part of reconnecting thousands of alumni of The Human Jukebox. We informed them of the needs of the current band and solicited assistance, while providing them with spaces to gather and reminisce on memories.

With the simple office of Recorder of Records being my first assignment, I quickly rose to the office of vice president, then the honorable position of the first female president of the HJAA! How ironic, not even ten years prior, I had been denied an audition to become a member of the band. One year later, I was sitting in the room with the largest female crab class. There were so many obstacles along the way. Here I was, a young woman from Mississippi, standing before hundreds of men to lead our alumni association. Throughout my time in leadership with the HJAA, I learned valuable life lessons on working with people from different eras and different backgrounds, and with conflicting thought processes and ideas. The good times were great, and the bad times were heavy. That experience taught me a lot about what type of leader I did, and did not, want to be. Under my leadership, we made great strides by providing book vouchers and tuition assistance to current students, providing prospective students with VIP Bayou Classic experiences, providing disaster relief to our members in need, purchasing new instruments and computers for the current students, and so much more.

One of my former professors and now great friend, makes a joke all the time that when I made it to Baton Rouge, I thought I was in New York City coming from Mississippi. The funny thing is that it was kind of like New York City to me! It was so new and full of opportunity. There was room for me to grow and come into my own. Upon graduating, I promised myself that I would forever support Southern any way I could. I owed that to Southern because they gave me an opportunity, starting with a postcard for a fall open house in 2003. The Jaguar Nation has been with me since the day I graduated. From attending the University of Tennessee at Chattanooga and being able to connect with some people who had Southern University ties, to relocating to College Station, Texas and finding a home with the Southern University Alumni Federation-Houston Chapter, Southern has provided me with many leadership opportunities. Ranging from becoming a member of the Southern University Young Alumni Network (SUYAN) Executive Board, to leading the HJAA, to mentoring students and working with many alumni committees and initiatives. The leadership opportunities have been plentiful, and I'm sure there are many more to come.

I will forever strive to find ways to rally the engagement of our alumni to stay connected and continually giving back to Southern University, who gave so much to us. It will always be my goal to implement ways to provide resources to the Southern University Marching Band program that changed my life forever. I contribute much of my *SUccess* to my education and experience gained at Southern University. It wasn't just what I learned in the classroom, but what I gained from the processes, the diverse backgrounds and cultures, and the heavy traditions that are instilled in a defender of the gold and blue. As I continue this journey of life, I often think of SU pioneers, such as Dr. Dolores Spikes. Her greatness, along with many more revered Jaguars, continues to push me forward in hopes of one day being amongst the ranks of Southernites with profound impact to the well-being and advancement of our beloved university. *"O Southern, dear Southern, we owe our all to thee."*

About Marissa Jones

Marissa M. Jones, MS, ATC, LAT is a native of Crystal Springs, MS. After graduating from Crystal Springs High School in 2005, she went on to attend Southern University and A&M College in Baton Rouge, LA. While there, she became a member of Sigma Alpha Iota Music Fraternity for Women (Spring '06) and the "often imitated, but never duplicated" Human Jukebox Marching Band. In addition to, within her major she served in leadership for the Therapeutic Recreation and Leisure Studies Society as well as a tutor. In May of 2009, Marissa graduated Magna Cum Laude with a Bachelor of Science in Therapeutic Recreation and Leisure Studies. Although presented with many job opportunities, Marissa re-visited her initial career goals of becoming an athletic trainer and went on to attend the University of Tennessee-Chattanooga, where she received her Master of Science in Athletic Training in May 2012 and became a nationally Certified Athletic Trainer (ATC).

Shortly after becoming an ATC, she accepted a job in College Station, TX as the DME Coordinator/Outreach Athletic Trainer for Central Texas Sports Medicine in College Station, TX. While continuing to serve as an outreach athletic trainer, she went on to serve as the first full time athletic trainer at Franklin ISD in Franklin, TX , where she worked building a comprehensive Sports Medicine program for 3 years. In 2016, Marissa decided to further her education by accepting an Athletic Training Residency specializing in Orthopedic Rehabilitation at Houston Methodist Sugar Land with a primary assignment to Thurgood Marshall High School in Missouri City, TX. Upon completion of the residency, she was hired full-time at Thurgood Marshall High School where she currently works as the Assistant Athletic Trainer and CTE Health Science teacher. Marissa has worked with a variety of athletes from Pee Wee to professionals; a variety of organizations including Texas A&M University, Louisiana State University, University of Alabama, Games of Texas, Football University and so on; a variety of sports including, but not limited to, football, basketball, ice hockey, lacrosse, women's semi-pro football, and rugby.

With a sincere passion for her alma mater, Marissa spends much of her free time engaging in many of its organizations and events. Previously, Marissa served as the first female and the 2nd President of the Human Jukebox Alumni Association (HJAA), where she is also a member of the Board of Trustees. During her tenure as President, the organization grew tremendously in membership, aided many students through financial assistance and mentoring, and provided a first of its kind Alumni Battle of the Bands between the Human Jukebox and Marching storm alumni bands which raised funds that were provided to their respective band programs to assist with needs of the current students. In addition to the HJAA, Marissa is an active Life Member of the Southern University Alumni Federation nationally and locally in Houston, TX. She has been a driving force in the Southern University Young Alumni Network (SUYAN) since its inception and currently serves as the co-chair of the Development and Fundraising committee and Houston representative. In 2019, Marissa was inducted into Southern University's 40 Under 40 Inaugural Cohort acknowledging her contributions to the community and Southern University. At any given time, you can find Marissa doing what she really loves, talking with students about their paths after high school and how to obtain their life goals.

One of Marissa's favorite things to do is TRAVEL! Whether to sporting events or out the country, she loves to pack her bags and go. Planning events and spending time with friends and family are high in the list of favorites. As a proud member of Delta Sigma Theta Sorority, Inc. (HMAC '19), Marissa spends a lot of time surveying the needs of the community and assisting in planning events and providing resources to address those needs. As a person that has had very influential women to help shape the person that she is today, Marissa takes mentoring very seriously and hopes to formalize her own mentoring program very soon.

Tramelle D. Howard, J.D.

Pure and True as the Gold and Blue
Tramelle D. Howard, J.D.

There is nothing quite like Baton Rouge, Louisiana. Oftentimes, it's a place that goes unnoticed because it's not a large city. However, it's the place I have called home since 1989. Baton Rouge has many exciting things that make it special, but nothing is quite more intriguing than being the home of the only HBCU system in the country. An HBCU system that has continued to run and operate, despite many challenges. The system is made up of five institutions across Louisiana. You cannot mention Baton Rouge without mentioning The Southern University system.

Growing up in Baton Rouge had its own set of unique challenges. But for a young, Black male, the potential of possibility always existed across the hump or through the back gates of Southern University. I grew up in a community called the field, or the avenues, as some folks refer to it. The field is located literally right outside the back gates of Southern University, so close that you can hear The Human Jukebox practicing from my front yard. My first introduction to Southern University was through the Southern University football program. I vividly remember going to watch the Jaguars on Saturday night in Mumford Stadium as my favorite pastime. I would wait in eager anticipation for football season each and every year. There were many traumatic things that occurred in my childhood but being on campus was the great escape.

There are no words to describe the level of excitement I experienced each and every opportunity I had to be on the yard. It was the one thing that the community would embrace and had so much pride in. No matter if you went to Southern or not, you knew that Southern belonged to us, and you took that to heart. My grandparents introduced me to Southern and neither of them graduated from the institution. But the love and dedication were second to none. One of my fondest memories of Southern University was having the opportunity to escort a Miss Southern University candidate during the Miss Southern pageant. When the PA announcer introduced me as the future football coach of Southern, I literally felt like the world was mine to conquer.

My formal education through the Southern University system began at the Southern University Laboratory school, a school that was built on the campus of Southern University to train teachers. At Southern Lab, it was like being the younger generation of Jaguars, who had the unique experience of attending grade school on a college campus. We could literally see Mumford Stadium across campus. We graduated in the same building that the college kids graduated in. Many of my favorite teachers, Ms. Watson, Ms. Aguillard, Ms. Green and Mr. Jones were students at Southern while teaching at Southern Lab. They looked after us and cared about our well-being. Southern University has always been that nurturing and caring place that educated wonderful people. Not only were they academically equipped, but they took the time to ensure that we were seen and could achieve anything we put our minds to. They made you feel like the smartest person in the world.

I also had the opportunity to be coached by Southern professors. Russell Jones was my mock trial coach. He also served as a professor in the law center. He pushed me like no other and believed in me often when I could not believe in myself. The moment came full circle when Professor Jones became my law school professor eight years after being my high school mock trial coach. It was quite the experience. It was provided by Southern University seeing a need and developing a solution. Southern University literally equipped me with the skills to change the trajectory of my life.

After graduating from Southern Lab, I went through some self-discovery. I wanted to leave Baton Rouge and see what else was out there. So, I attended college away. I always knew I would return to Southern in some capacity, but I never knew what capacity. I ended up back at Southern by way of the Southern University Law Center. My Southern Law experience was truly second to none. I can't think of any other institution that would have afforded me such an amazing legal educational experience. The family environment, the level of nurture and care, and the sense of belonging will be something I'll forever cherish. I was able to actualize my goals, dreams and aspirations. It was all because Southern University gave a young man from the avenues access to opportunity. Southern believed in me when many others turned their backs. For that, I'm forever grateful. I was pushed to the limit and challenged to reach my full potential. I had the opportunity to take part in some unique experiences. I felt like my voice was heard, and I met some lifelong friends who have forever impacted my life.

To this day, I am still actively involved with the Southern University Alumni Federation. I am a current Southern Alumni Leadership cohort member, a season ticket holder for SU football, and **referred** to by many of my friends and family as "Lacumba" the mascot of our institution. Southern University changed my life, and it continues to play a significant role in my life. I'm forever grateful for the opportunities that have been afforded to me by Southern University. I'm forever grateful for the many doors Southern has opened for me. As pure and true as the gold and blue, I will forever sing the praises of Southern University.

I will always be loyal to a place that has singlehandedly changed my life.

About Tramelle D. Howard, J.D.

Tramelle Howard is an educator, community advocate and a deep believer in the urgent need to advance equity in all of its forms across every context.

Tramelle was raised by a single mother who, despite never attending college, embodied and demonstrated the transformative power of hard work and commitment—working multiple jobs to ensure the family had what it needed.

Similarly, his maternal grandfather, who attended school only until 9th grade, instilled in Tramelle and his siblings an unyielding belief that education can change and save lives. Tramelle credits that commitment to education for saving his life, helping to lift him and his siblings from poverty and build successful careers.

A Baton Rouge native, in 2018, Tramelle became the youngest person ever elected to the East Baton Rouge ("EBR") Parish School Board. Shortly after taking office, he was installed by his fellow members as Vice President of the Board.

As Vice President of the EBR School Board, he has been a champion for disadvantaged students and led the creation and adoption of EBR's first charter school accountability policy— ensuring that schools are first and foremost serving the best interests of students and that students receive a quality education. Tramelle has also been a champion for teacher diversity and elevating student voice.

Tramelle began his professional journey in education as an eighth-grade history teacher, serving with Teach for America South Louisiana after graduating with a Juris Doctor degree from Southern University Law Center.

It was while working in the Law Center's student family law clinic that his belief in the primacy of education in shaping life trajectories was reaffirmed. There, his clients were largely children of color facing financial hardship and trauma and bearing the weight of the failures of an inequitable public education system.

He saw in the faces and spirit of those young people the potential of hope amidst deprivation and struggle. He also heard the calling to do more—to work to empower young people facing the most barriers to success and ensure all students have access to a high-quality education.

Tramelle is currently the Louisiana External Relations and Policy Manager for Education Trust, a national nonprofit that works to close opportunity gaps that disproportionately affect students of color and students from low-income families. In that role, Tramelle is responsible for managing coalition work, policy implementation and building community partnerships across the state.

Candice A. Battiste, J.D.

Seriousness of Purpose: The Southern University Law Center
Candice A. Battiste, J.D.

I knew after my undergraduate experience of attending a predominantly white institution, my most sought-after dream of obtaining a law degree would need to come from an HBCU. The more I learned about racism, systemic discrimination in education, and systemic discrimination in policy, I knew the HBCU experience would be valuable as I navigated politics post-graduation. I thoroughly love south Louisiana. I was already familiar with the Southern University system while I attended undergraduate across the city at LSU. Upon learning of my acceptance to the Southern University Law Center, I was elated to know I would become a part of the harrowed tradition of attorneys, politicians, educators and business leaders who matriculated through the law school on "the Bluff."

The history of Southern University Law Center was born out of fellow African-American students who sought the law as a means of making positive change. As explained on the official website of Southern University Law Center:

"On December 16, 1946, in response to a lawsuit by an African-American resident seeking to attend law school at a state institution, the Louisiana State Board of Education took "positive steps to establish a Law School for Negroes at Southern University...to be in operation for the 1947-1948 session."

Plans for the law school were approved by the State Board of Education at its January 10, 1947 meeting. On June 14, 1947, the Board of Liquidation of State Debt appropriated $40,000 for the operation of the school. The Southern University Law School was officially opened in September 1947 to provide legal education for African-American students.

Southern University Law Center graduates, beginning with the legendary civil rights attorney, political leader and educator Jesse N. Stone, Jr., Alvin Basile Jones, Leroy White, Ellyson Fredrick Dyson, and Alex Louis Pitcher of the class of 1950, have spread across the state and nation as trailblazers in the legal profession, securing equal rights for many. To date, the Law Center has more than 2,500 graduates and is one of the nation's most racially diverse law schools.

After thirty-eight years of operation as a School of Law, the Southern University Board of Supervisors re-designated the school as the Southern University Law Center, enhancing its image in the region and the nation. The Law Center stresses legal education of high quality for students from diverse backgrounds.

"Seriousness of Purpose" was the slogan emblazoned across the atrium as we walked into the law school on our first day. From that initial day I came across the motto, it has remained with me. I carry it with me in everything I do. The beauty of attending law school at an HBCU was having professors who understood the challenges we would face in our careers as African Americans. Regardless of the prestige of a juris doctorate, we were fully aware that the evil of racism was still present. Our professors spent the three years they had us in their classrooms teaching us the history of the legal system, the law, and how we as Black students would continue a time-honored tradition of accepting the responsibility of progressing ourselves and communities forward.

Trayvon Martin was murdered the same year I entered law school. It was an ever-present reminder that the American legal system required evolving if we are to witness true, consistent justice. Professor Donald North is the professor who affirmed I was in the right place when I boldly stated that I disagreed with a legal opinion presented in our textbook. His concise statement, "If you disagree, then you're in the right place after all" taught me that an established legal opinion is not impervious to analysis and critique.

Attending an HBCU during those three years exposed me fully to the health disparities that plague communities who did not have equitable access to healthcare. Whether from a lack of health insurance prior to Medicaid expansion, the devastation of mortality rates for Black mothers and the families left behind, reproductive justice initiatives, which negatively impact women of color, the stigmatization of mental health issues in our community, and the intersections of misogyny, homophobia and racism. Meeting students from all walks of life contributed to the collective experience of what it means to exist as a Black person in America.

But attending an HBCU also further helped me appreciate the beauty of Black joy. From the first blare of a trumpet when listening to The Human Jukebox, to witnessing "pretty Wednesdays" when the sidewalks and cafeterias became catwalks, and the pride we feel when a celebrity 'reps' the Blue and Gold. Black pain may have been our undesired, undeserved birthright. But attending the Southern University Law Center made me realize it does not have to be our legacy.

Fellow students who would become my lifelong friends discussed the current events and marveled at the privilege of earning juris doctorate degrees in a space where we could show up as our whole selves. We knew the importance of continuing to cultivate spaces like that after graduation for those who supported our dreams and looked like us back home. We experienced a safe space in our everyday lives in those three years where Black folks could confidently, unapologetically exist. Once you have experienced home in fellow students, and an institution as rich as Southern, you do not forget it. You want everyone to know what it is like to have that.

As I proudly enter my fourth year of policy analysis, community organizing and political consulting work, I know it is because of the lessons learned at my HBCU that helped shape who I am. Law school at the Southern University Law Center taught me to embrace my leadership skills, approach adversity head on, and to center and magnify the voices of those who are historically marginalized and ignored in the halls and at the tables of civic engagement. In a time when the Voting Rights Act has been chipped away at, leaving many without a proper avenue to access the power constitutionally afforded to them, I will remember the motto I first saw as I walked into the sunlit atrium of the law school on the bluff: *Seriousness of Purpose*. That purpose may differ from one graduate to another, but we continue to unapologetically, tenaciously approach our futures, and the futures of those we touch, with seriousness and pride.

About Candice A. Battiste, J.D.

Candice Battiste is the North Louisiana organizer for the Power Coalition for Equity and Justice. She is an alum of Louisiana State University and earned her juris doctorate from Southern University Law Center. There, she served as President of Law Students for Reproductive Justice and was a recipient of the prestigious Marshall-Brennan Constitutional Literacy Fellowship. Upon graduation, Candice helped form the Family Law Unit of Legal Services of North Louisiana.

She was the past Shreveport-Bossier Field organizer with the Unanimous Jury Coalition/Yes On 2 campaign, serves on the Citizen SHE Board of Directors, the ACLU of Louisiana Board of Directors, Board of the Shreveport Downtown Development Authority and was selected as a United Nations Association Delegate. This past year she was selected as one of Shreveport's 40 Under 40. When Candice is not discussing progressive initiatives and working to affect positive change, she is traveling or can be found at one of Louisiana's many food and music festivals.

Jamal Donaldson Briggs

Called to Make A Way
Jamal Donaldson Briggs

O Southern, Dear Southern, thy praises we shall sing,
Until all the heavens and echoes loudly ring.
The winds and the sky as they pass us by
Will adoration bring.

O Southern, Dear Southern, we owe our all to thee.
In downfall or vict'ory, we'll always loyal be.
Thy sons and daughters as they work,
Will be inspired by thee.

O Southern, Dear Southern, thy name will ever be,
As mighty as the rivers that flow on to the sea,
As pure and true as the Gold and Blue,
That stand out bold for thee.

I will always stand boldly and profess my love for my fair alma mater. Like so many over the past 141 years, I found my voice and place in the world on this venerable, transformative school on the Scott's Bluff. Southern University and Agricultural & Mechanical College is both my home and my dream deferred.

I remember being an ambitious eighteen-year-old, taking my first flight and arriving at Baton Rouge Metro Airport alone. I was the first person in my family go to college. My village was beaming with pride, but it was a lonesome experience. My late grandmother often said, "That boy is going to be somebody if it kills him." My grandmother's words were almost prophetic. Coming from Western New York during the heatwave of 1998 proved to be taxing on my body. I suffered sun stroke and spent most of the semester at Baton Rouge General Hospital. Our Vice Chancellor of Student Affairs was supportive, knowing that I was 1,750 miles away from home and was adamant about staying. Weeks later, I received a phone call from Chancellor Jackson, who said that he had, "heard about this kid from New York who kept ending up in the hospital and refused to go home." He said, "Son, you will always be a Southern Jaguar. Please go home and take care of your health."

I went back home. I enrolled in community college. I took care of myself and, shortly thereafter, I took care of my grandmother, who had a massive stroke. I wanted to return to Southern, but my doctors advised against it. I chose the University of North Carolina at Charlotte. In eighteen months, I graduated as class president. I learned on the morning of my graduation that my grandmother was diagnosed with terminal endometrial cancer. She hid it from me because she wanted to see me finish school. Devastated, I stood with resolve, delivering the class address while I held back tears, looking at the seat the chancellor kept empty in her honor. I was awarded the university's inaugural Leadership Medal. In a final salute, I placed the medal in her hands before closing her casket. One thing life has taught me is *resilience*!

While I am many things, good and bad, I am foremost a Southern University and A&M College Jaguar. As we are enjoying this resurgent renaissance of HBCUs in light of the tumultuous summer of 2020, the world is finding out what we already knew: our experience is more than the accumulation of credits. It is a collective experience where we were unapologetically affirmed in our race and ethnicity and equipped with the tools to be successful in the America that we aspire her to be. Southern is much more than my alma mater. It is my home! I haven't been on campus in over twenty years, but it remains my refuge.

I am thrilled to return to my alma mater as a candidate for the Executive Ph.D. in Public Policy at the Nelson Mandela College of Government and Social Sciences. This is my Sankofa moment. 'Sankofa' is expressed in the Akan language as "se wo were fi na wosan kofa a yenki." The literal translation is, "It is not taboo to go back and fetch what you forgot." Sankofa teaches us that we must go back to our roots in order to move forward. Like our college's namesake, he began his academic career at the University College of Fort Hare, where he was later expelled for participating in a student protest. But he went back to the University of Fort Hare after studying at the University of South Africa.

Admittedly, I all but abandoned my dreams of returning to Southern and earning the Ph.D. However, I am undoubtedly prepared to work to make both a reality. I am a witness of the transformative power that institutions of higher education possess in achieving a fair, equitable and just society. I aspired to be a provost at a major research university. The ability to make an impact on systems fuels my passion. I had the opportunity to contribute to the sustainability of two urban research universities, but it ain't home!

This is a literal homecoming! The Executive Ph.D. in Public Policy at Southern University and A&M College is more than a terminal degree. It is the answering of my life's call and the summation of my life work as a scholar-practitioner. The needs of our community are too pervasive. This program requires one to be passionate about solving a problem, as opposed to simply contributing to research literature. If I am accepted, I will focus my attention on equity gaps in higher education funding. I remember being a freshman at Southern. I was so excited to be there! I also remember the sinking feeling I had after going to LSU's campus. I am well aware that the Southern University System and the Louisiana State University System are quite different. Nevertheless, after seeing both flagship campuses, the vestiges of segregation and inequitable funding rocked me to my core!

History matters. The study of HBCUs is not new. There aren't enough of us telling our stories and making policy. The Executive Ph.D. affords me the opportunity to fill that void. I intend to incorporate history into public policy analysis because it is imperative in having a firm grasp and comprehensive understanding of complex policy issues. The disparities between Jaguarland and Tigerland go back as far as 1890 with the Louisiana Legislature setting the legal precedent of the unfulfilled "Separate but Equal" doctrine. In applying historical thinking to public policy, one is able to see that publicly funded HBCUs have been subjected to centuries of systemic racism coupled with inefficient business and fundraising practices that resulted in institutions that are weaker financially than many predominantly white institutions. Research literature indicates that HBCUs rely more heavily on federal, state and local resources than other institutions. I am captivated by the resiliency of these venerable institutions and their collective ability to thrive in the face of adversity.

Further, true to our mission as a land grant institution. I plan to conduct research on the role of the nineteen public land grant HBCUs and PBIs (Predominately Black Institutions) in addressing food insecurity. There is growing research that indicates how prevalent food insecurity is among college students and the strong correlation between their well-being and educational experience. A majority of the "1890 institutions", named for the year they were incorporated into the U.S. Department of Agriculture's land-grant program, are located in low-income, rural areas, where the closest grocery store is at least five miles away. As a policy analyst, I saw my eighteen-year-old self, trying to walk that hump to go to the corner store. Suffice it to say, I made friends with cars quickly!

I subscribe to the belief that, "Charity starts at home and spreads abroad." Southern University and A&M College is the place that will always be home. From the "Baddest Band in the Land" to the red beans and rice on Mondays for lunch and those fine AKAs, Southern is a place where I learned to love myself. It is almost a magical place that affirmed the best of me and challenged me to become my best self.

Since 1880, my fair alma mater answered the call to simply make a way in the face of adversity and peril. As a Southern Jaguar, I am ecstatic to come home and make my beloved Jaguarland better than I found it.

About Jamal Donaldson Briggs

Jamal Donaldson Briggs began his career in Office of Senator Hillary Clinton where he transitioned as a program evaluation consultant with the U.S. Department of Education and the U.S. Department of Health and Human Services. He is currently a Process Design Consultant at Bank of America's Center for Operational Expertise based in Plano, Texas.

Jamal is very active in the service-learning movement being heavily involved in the development of the City/County Youth Council in his hometown of Rochester, NY which developed more than 20 workshops around leadership development and team building for youth. He was a Learn-N-Serve America Peer Mentor providing peer-based training & technical assistance with implementing service-learning programs in schools K-16.

Jamal served on the project design team for The Rochester Children's Zone (RCZ), a community planning initiative designed to develop a comprehensive and holistic approach to improving educational outcomes for children in the Northeast neighborhood of Rochester, New York which is home to some of the poorest zip codes in the country. Jamal is a founding member of Clinton Global Initiative-University, which convenes college student around the world to devise and implement innovative solutions to pressing global challenges.

Jamal prides himself as scholar-practitioner. He obtained the Bachelor of Arts in political science degree from the University of North Carolina at Charlotte where he was named a Ronald E. McNair Post-Baccalaureate Achievement Scholar. Jamal also pursued theological education at Duke University Divinity School. He graduated from Northeastern University with a Master of Science degree in leadership and health management. Jamal is also an executive education fellow at Harvard Kennedy School.

At UNC Charlotte, he was active in student government serving as student body provost and senior class president. Jamal was the architect of the University's academic honor code, midterm course evaluation pilot project and *Conversations in Leadership* distinguished lecture series. In his capacity as Vice President of

Academic Affair for the UNC System Association of Student Governments, Jamal played an integral role in advocating and implementing a 4-year tuition hike cap with System President Erskine Bowles.

His scholarly work on religion and politics was presented at the American Political Science Association, American Academy of Religion and the prestigious Henry Institute Biennial Symposium on Religion and Politics. Jamal's various works was published in the *Encyclopedia of Political Science. African-American National Biography, The Oxford Encyclopedia of African American History 1895 – Present, Reforming America: A Thematic Encyclopedia and Document Collection of the Progressive Era* and *Arts & Humanities Leadership: A Reference Guide.*

Jamal has over 12 years of experience in political organizing and leadership development. He was the Charlotte Area Coordinator with New Baptist Covenant and is active with the National Urban League Young Professionals. He served as a Deputy Director of the Young Democrats of America's Faith & Values Initiative, Chair of the Policy and Platform Committee of Young Democrats of America Minority Caucus. Most recently, he served on the Deputy Director of African-American Faith Outreach for Hillary for America, a DNC Faith Outreach Team member and was Assistant to the Deputy Executive Director for External Relations for the Charlotte In 2012 Convention Host Committee.

Jamal is Co-Founder and Vice Chair of The SafeChild Foundation, Inc. and serves on the Advisory Boards of the Novo Community Foundation, UNC Charlotte College of Liberal Arts & Sciences; UNC Charlotte Center for Professional and Applied Ethics; American Association of Caregiving Youth; *Harvard Business Review and* Development Dimensions International, Inc. (DDI) Solutions Advisory Board.

Jamal's honors include the President's Student Service Award by President William J. Clinton; UNC Charlotte's Distinguished Leadership Medal; the Dr. James H and Martha H Woodward Distinguished Service Award; and an acknowledgement in *Who's Who Among American College and University Students.*

Jonas Vanderbilt

Leaving a Legacy
Jonas Vanderbilt

Taking that first journey across the famous bridge known as "the hump" is one journey that every alumnus of Southern University and A&M College can certainly attest to. It represents a new beginning. From the views of the famous A.W. Mumford Stadium to the beautiful sun shining off the waves on the bluff of the mighty Mississippi River, the aesthetic beauty of the Jaguar Nation's home is breathtaking. Coming from the small town of New Iberia, Louisiana, my mind couldn't fathom what I was in store for. Encouraged by my sister, a then USL student and a neighborhood friend, Tyra Davis, I was HBCU bound rather than attending a predominantly white institution. Being a musician and drum major, I was attracted by the number one band in the country, "The Human Jukebox." Little did I know, my life would begin again on "The Yard" and the start to building my legacy had bloomed.

Being dropped off one Sunday afternoon for band camp at the legendary, now known as Isaac Greggs Band Hall for that first late-night session, was the first of challenges to overcome. A long night of auditioning and shaving off every curl on my head gave birth to a new man. Early mornings and extremely late nights with The Human Jukebox upperclassmen and icons such as Greggs, Lawrence Jackson, Carnell Knighten and Goose was the beginning of building the character and professional I am today. Being a native of New Iberia yielded ties to another yet influential person and longtime friend "Mr. Drum Major Sir" Terral "Too Cold" Jackson, Jr. His father was from the same city as myself and my great friend and roommate, his protégé, "Tre Jay" Scott Boutte. This led us to being a part of a hand-selected group of crabs to learn much more than we bargained for. This ultimately gave me much insight and connections to many other students in which have all left our legacies at our institution.

I came from a fun-loving, dancing family. Starting a small group in high school with other friends, we performed for many local events and concerts. This led me to having the confidence to display these talents and also become one of the lead choreographers for the band's most legendary dance routines, Super 7. It even led to assisting the Fabulous Dancing Dolls. Having no formal training, I watched the dancers perform and, after two takes, was able to emulate. Being a freshman at the time, we performed many skits. This created a way into the dance realm and opened the door to connections with my crab sisters (only fellow freshman dancers because at that time there was only one female in the band). This ultimately led to meeting and learning from legendary dancers such as Kiki-Ely, a friend and now choreographer/director to the stars, as well as being inspired by the likes of Traci Prince, a professional dancer in the industry and one of the most influential changemakers of dance at Southern. I came to SU as a chemistry major. Yet, I continued to pursue this field of entertainment called dance because, after a brief year and a half, I started serving as instructor. Showing my professionalism, always being a hard worker, and catapulting a dance career led to the admiration of my talents for the head band directors to follow Greggs. I choreographed much for the band program and legendary dancers. This was a God-given talent. Being a part of this organization led me to not only discovering it, but also mastering it.

In the band, I met Mike "Kennybone" McLaughlin. At the time, I thought he was an evil upperclassman. He later became not only my S-Phi brother, but also my roommate and line brother along with twenty-two other game changers. As roommates and friends, we maneuvered our way into the likeness of the admired and statured Nupes of the "Mothership Chapter of the Southwestern Province." So many stories can be told of our days. Yet, in the spring of 1999, I pledged the Alpha Sigma Chapter of Kappa Alpha Psi, Fraternity, Inc. with him. The life lessons, experiences, development and maturity of a collegian joining that chapter are endless. Blessed to be granted access to this unbreakable bond of brothers is a highlight of a chosen few of the campus.

That year of Greek life at SU was a legendary year. As the new members of each of the NPHC organizations, we set the tone for what Greek life was to become. The fact that many of us were friends beforehand left a legacy of comradery and a passion for excellence with new programming, creative award-winning step shows, and ultimately, the family vibe that is SU NPHC. Programming such as "Meet the Greeks" which later evolved into the Divine Intervention Program began under my leadership as a Director of Student Life. This program has now been instituted on at least five other HBCU campuses. It enhances knowledge, growth and responsibility for one of the biggest recruitment tools for an institution: Greek life. In that role, I was able to institute so many practices and social norms that have now become the essence of what student life is at SU. Advising and setting the pace for many other colleges to follow, the infamous royal court's style, presence and coronations, SGA's practices and presence, and Nupes of the campus' programming, creativity and movement set a high bar. I have choreographed, helped create and/ or conducted a production of program for every NPHC organization.

One of the biggest contributions to the university and legacy left would be the Gold'N Bluez Dance Team. Formerly, the university had the Fastbreak Dancers of the 80s and the Jaguar Jems of the late 90s. Creating a new team was a challenge. Changing the culture and mindsets of our people in that era was no small feat. Yet, setting a bar, finding the uniqueness and education factor as to the normalcy of it at other bigger institutions, I kept up the fight. Since its conception, the team has become a major part of the national dance world. They have competed in such conferences as the Black College National Cheer and Dance Team Championships to choreographing and staffing camps for various colleges and high schools. As a student at the time, I envisioned an opportunity for more than the traditional nine plus females on the campus to be able to represent their university by displaying their passion, skill and talents for the world to see. As a mixture of the styles of various basketball teams, stage and Broadway feels, mixed with the flare of the southern and SWAC norms, me and dance friends molded a powerhouse. The team is a hard-working organization of the university that participates in many community events, as well as campus functions. have won various awards and accolades and has held the title of SWAC Dance Team Champions for three years. They have been featured at the 2010-19 Bayou Classic Greek Shows, danced with various celebrities opening pre-game shows, and other celebrity and industry music videos, productions and television films. Not only dancers for the university, the Gold'N Bluez are also the basketball dancers. They perform at every home game, all homecoming events, fall and spring student events, as well as some away games. The team is utilized as a huge recruiting tool and traveling showcase for engagement and recruitment efforts. I have produced a multitude of NBA, NFL, AFL, professional dancers, and studio owners, with over 250 dancers since its conception. Creating this opportunity for women to represent their institution, and create a family, has been the paramount highlight of my years at SU. I'd be remiss not to mention that my entire professional dance career and this team would have not been possible without the push from renowned Cheer Coach James Smith, Sr. to present my talent to the world. He voluntold me to compete in my first professional competition at Black College Nationals, where I won first place. That was the confidence booster and the support I needed then, and he still gives to this date.

Being an alumnus of the institution, which I now work for, presented many challenges. Yet, I do not regret many at all. Working for twelve years at Southern University also shaped my professional career. Having Terral Jackson, Sr. and Tracie Abraham take a chance on a young kid, and give me my first opportunity, led me back into the cycle and shaping. I molded many presidents, leaders, dancers and students to state leaders, professional dancers and actors, entrepreneurs and bosses in their own right. I have also created lifelong friendships and family during my tenure at Southern. Some would say we were the gatekeepers of the office and my protective crew. Working under several bosses helped mold me into the person I am today. Yet, one catapulted me even further. Dr. Brandon K. Dumas, through tough love and a journey to ultimately a brotherhood, allowed me to experience the professional side of student affairs by exposing and pushing my journey and membership to several professional organizations. Rearing many students to their highest potential, I instinctively followed that model, building many students and drawing out their passions and potential.

One note that should be a takeaway for any professional is to humbly work hard and strive to be the best at whatever job level you find yourself. This connection led to the melding of a powerhouse team. Alongside my other SU legendary, former student, talented best friend, and colleague Shaquille "Shaq" Dillon, my then boss took me to my next professional destination, where we created a legacy and new traditions where I am climbing up the ladder to a destiny not yet determined. Consequently, being a former SU undergraduate student, soon to be three-time graduate, and former employee, who took full advantage of and poured back into your secondary home known as college, *SUccess* is eminent!

About Jonas Owen Vanderbilt Jr., M.Ed.

Jonas Owen Vanderbilt Jr., M.Ed., currently serving as the Assistant Vice President for Student Affairs at Wiley College, has in his previous capacity, at his alma mater Southern University, served as a Program Director for the Student Union, Coordinator for Student Programs, and most recent the Director for Student Life has a 13-year work history in Student Affairs. Aside from vast budgeting experience, he has been responsible for all Special Events, Greek Life, Student Leadership, Organizations, Career Services and Auxiliary Groups for which he coached, created, and choreographed.

Two of his years at his previous institution of employment, Mr. Vanderbilt served as an Adjunct Professor acquainting the first year experience students with the university and assisted with the transitioning of those individuals and their career development. After obtaining his Bachelor of Science in Chemistry, he also acquired a Master's in Educational Leadership as well from Southern University and A&M College. An active member, Mr. Vanderbilt was initiated at the Alpha Sigma Chapter of Kappa Alpha Psi Fraternity, Incorporated where he served as an advisor for many years catapulting his undergraduate chapter to multiple Chapter of the Year and individual awards as well as earned a multitude of city recognitions while living in Baton Rouge, Louisiana.

Being a part of several professional organizations such as Higher Education and Leadership Foundation (HELF) staff and Iota Cohort member, Association for Fraternity and Sorority Advisors (AFA), National Association for Student Affairs Professionals (NASAP), Student Affairs Professionals in Higher Education (NASPA), Association for the Promotion of Campus Activities (APCA), and National Society for Leadership and Success (NSLS), he has proven a servant of all as well as a master of his crafts, as an instructor and presenter of management , event planning, choreography, greek life and student leadership development.

Official Partners & Sponsors of the HBCU Experience Movement, LLC

Baker & Baker Realty, LLC
Christopher Baker- CEO/Founder
Instagram: seedougieblake
Facebook: Christopher D. Baker
Email: baker.christopher@gmail.com

HBCU Buzz
LUKE LAWAL JR.
lawal@lcompany.co
Fndr, CEO | (301) 221-1719 @lukelawal
L & COMPANY { *HBCU Buzz* | *Taper, Inc.* |
Root Care Health }

Bound By Conscious Concepts
Kathryn Lomax-CEO/Founder
Instagram: msklovibes223
Facebook: Klo-Kathryn Lomax
Contact: (972) 638-9823
Email: Klomax@bbconcepts.com

Zoom Technologies, LLC
Torrence Reed - CEO/Founder
Instagram: torrencereed3
Email: support@zoom-technologies.co

Dancer NC Dance District
Dr. Kellye Worth Hall
Instagram: divadoc5
Facebook: Kellye Worth Hall
Email: delta906@gmail.com

Yard Talk 101
Jahliel Thurman CEO/Founder
Instagram: YardTalk101
Website: YardTalk101.com

HBCU Wall Street
Torrence Reed & Jamerus Peyton-
CEO/Founders
Facebook: HBCU Wall Street
Email: info@hbcuwallstreet.com

Springbreak Watches (SPGBK)
Kwame Molden- CEO/Founder
Instagram: SPGBK
Facebook: Kwame Molden
Email: info@springbreakwatches.com

Minority Cannabis Business Association
Shanita Penny- President
Instagram- Minority Cannabis
Facebook- MCBA.Org
Twitter- MinCannBusAssoc
LinkedIn- Minority Cannabis Business
Association
Email-info@minoritycannabis.org
Website: www.MinorityCannabis.org
Phone: 202-681-2889

The Phoenix Professional Network
DJavon Alston-Owner/Founder
Instagram: thephoenixnetwork757
Facebook: DJavon Alston
Email: thephoenixnetwork757@gmail.com

Chef Batts
Keith Batts-CEO/Founder
Instagram: chefbatts
Email: booking@chefbatts.com

Johnson Capital
Marcus Johnson CEO/Founder
Instagram: marcusdiontej
Email: marcus@johnsoncap.com

SheIsMagazine
CEO/Founder: Ciara Horton
Instagram:@sheisemagazine
Facebook:Ciara Horton
Email: ciarasheisemagazine.com

Success and Religion
CEO/Founder: Micheal Taylor
Email: Successismyreligion@gmail.com

Never2Fly2Pray
Jeffrey Lee Sawyer: Owner/Founder
Instagram: never2fly2pray
Facebook: Jeffrey Lee
Email htdogwtr@yahoo.com

Queen Series
CEO/Founder: Randall Barnes
Email: aqueenseries@gmail.com

Allen Financial Solutions
Jay Allen: Owner/Founder
Instagram: jay83allen
Facebook: Jay Allen
Email: allen.jonathan83@gmail.com

HBCU Girls Talk
CEO/Founder: TeeCee Camper
Instagram: @hbcugirlstalk
Contact: talkgirls@yahoo.com

Holistic Practitioners
Tianna Bynum: CEO/Founder
Facebook: Tianna Bynum
Email tpb33@georgetown.edu

VJR Real Estate
CEO/Founder: Victor Collins, Jr.
Instagram: vjrtherealtor
Email Address: Vic@TheVJRGroup.com

Journee Enterprises
Fred Whit: CEO/Founder
Facebook: Fred Whit
Instagram: frederickwjr
Email: frederickwjr@yahoo.com

Company: Ashley Little Enterprises, LLC
Ashley Little- CEO/Founder
Facebook: Ashley Little
Instagram: _ashleyalittle
Email: aalittle08@gmail.com
www.ashleylittleenterprises.com

HBCU Pride Nation
CEO/ Founder: Travis Jackson
Instagram: hbcupridenation
Facebook: HBCU Pride Nation
Email: travispjackson@gmail.com

LK Productions
CEO/Founder: Larry King
Instagram: lk_rrproduction
Facebook: Larry King
Email: lk_production@yahoo.com

STAMP'D TRAVEL
CEO/Founder: Jocelyn Hadrick Alexander
Instagram: @jocehadyou
Website: www.stampdtravel.com
Email Address:
Jocelyn.h.alexander@gmail.com

ICG Marriage & Family Therapy
CEO/Founders: Jabari & Stephanie Walthour
Instagram: @thedopesextherapist
Website: www.intimacycenterga.com
Email Address:
stephanie@intimacycenterga.com

Electikread Marketing
CEO/Founder: Christa Newkirk
Instgram:@chris_ta_da
Email Address: info@eclectikread.com

NXLEVEL TRAVEL (NXLTRVL)
Chief Executive Officer Hercules Conway
Chief Operating Officer Newton Dennis
Instagram-nxlevel
Instagram: herc3k
Facebook-Newton Dennis
Facebook: Hercules Conway
Email Address: info@nxleveltravel.com
Website: NXLEVELTRAVEL.COM

SHANI L.
Relationship Enthusiast
Website: www.shanilfarmer.com
Instagram: @shanilrelationshipenthusiast
Email Address: info@shanilfarmer.com

BLKWOMENHUSTLE
CEO/Founder: Lashawn Dreher
Instagram: blkwomenhustle
Facebook: Blk Women Hustle
Email: info@blkwomenhustle.com

The Alli Group, LLC
Real Estate Management
Lawrence & Nickia Alli
Website: www.thealligroupllc.com
Instagram: @thealligroupllc
Email Address: nickia.alli@gmail.com

HBCU Grad
CEO/Founder Todd Finley
www.hbcugraduates.com
312-535-8511

Upward Path
CEO/Founder: Cameron Chalmers Dupree
Website: www.upwardpathtc.com
Instagram: @upwardpathtc
Email Address: contact@upwardpathtc.com

Campaign Engineers
Chris Smith, CEO/Founder
Instagram: csmithatl
Email Address: csmith1911@gmail.com

Boardroom Brand LLC
Samuel Brown III, CEO/Founder
Instagram: _gxxdy
Email Address:
samuel.brown.three@gmail.com

HBCU 1010
Jahliel Thurman, CEO/Founder
www.hbcu101.com
Instagram: hbcu101
jahlielthurman@gmail.com

Uplift Clothing Apparel
Jermaine Simpson, CEO/Founder
UpliftClothingApparel.com
Instagram: Upliftclothingapparel

The Vernon Group Cooperative Solutions
CEO/Founder: Anthony V. Stevens
Instagram: @investednu
Email Address: info@vernongroupllc.com

LEMM Media Group
CEO/Founder: Cremel Nakia Burney
Instagram: @cremel_the_creator
Email Address: cremelburney@gmail.com

PILAR

PILAR
Co-Owner: Nate Perry
Instagram: @barpilar
Email Address: nate@pilardc.com

AC Events The Luxury Planning Experience
Amy Agbottah, CEO/Founder:
Email Address: amy@amycynthiaevents.com

HBCU Pulse
CEO/Founder Randall Barnes
Website: hbcupulse.com
Instagram: @hbcupulse
Twitter: @thehbcupulse

According To RP Podcast
CEO/Founder: Ritha Pierre, Esq.
Instagram: @accordingtorp
Email Address: accordingtorp@gmail.com

SwagHer
Vice President Of Sales/Marketing Jarmel
Roberson
Website www.swagher.net
instagram: swaghermagazine
Email Address: jroberson@swagher.net

Freedas World Podcast
CEO/Founder: Ritha Pierre, Esq.
Instagram: @freedas_world
Email Address: accordingtorp@gmail.com

Janea Jamison, Host/Creator
H.E.R. Story, LLC
IG: @herstory_podcast
Facebook: HER STORY Podcast
https://soundcloud.com/herstorypod
Email: herstory89llc@gmail.com
Phone: (504) 224-9669

HBCU CHEER BLACK EXCELLENCE
Instagram: @HBCUCheer
Email: HBCUcheerleaders@yahoo.com

HBCU Buzz
LUKE LAWAL JR.
lawal@lcompany.co
Fndr, CEO | (301) 221-1719 @lukelawal
L & COMPANY { *HBCU Buzz | Taper, Inc.* |
Root Care Health }

February First
CEO/Founder: Cedric Livingston
www.februaryfirstmovie.com
Director/Writer February First: A Stride
Towards Freedom

HBCU Times
David Staten, Ph.
hbcutimes@gmail.com
Facebook: HBCU Times
Instagram: hbcu_times8892
Bridget Hollis Staten, Ph.D

Swing Into Their Dreams Foundation
Pamela Parker and Lynn Demmons, Co-
Founders
Email Address:
swingintotheirdreams@gmail.com
Website: swingintotheirdreams.com

The Lady BUGS
CEO/Founder: Tatiana Tinsley Dorsey
Instagram: @theladybugsofficial
Email Address:
ladybugs_HQ@googlegroups.com

OEDM Group
CEO/Principal Owner: Justin Blake
Website: www.oedmgroup.com
Instagram: @oedmgroup.com
Email Address: contact@oedmgroup.com

SayYes

Say Yes, LLC
CEO/Founder: Porscha Lee Taylor
Website: www.sayyesplanners.com
Instagram: @sayyesplanners
Email Address: info@sayyescareer.com

Harbor Institute
CEO/Founder: Rasheed Ali Cromwell, JD
Instagram: @theharborinstitute
Facebook: The Harbor Institute
Twitter: @harborinstitute
Email: racromwell@theharborinstitute.com

Marching Sport
CEO/Founder: Gerard Howard
Email Address:
gerardhoward@gmail.com

THE HBCU
BAND
EXPERIENCE
WITH CHRISTY WALKER

The HBCU Band Experience with
Christy Walker
CEO/Founder: Dr. Christy Walker
Email Address:
christywalker57@gmail.com
Website:
http://www.christyawalker.com

Reid Creative Solutions, LLC
CEO/Founder: Aja Reid
info@reidcreativesolutions.com
Phone: (919) 822-2892
www.reidcreativesolutions.com

Vision Tree LLC
CEO/Founder: Dr. Jorim Reed
visiontreellc@gmail.com

Kelly Collaborative

Kelly Collaborative Medicine
CEO/Founder: Dr. Kathryn Kelly
10801 Lockwood Drive, Suite 160
Silver Spring, MD 20901
(301) 298-1040
www.kellymedicinemd.com

Brooks Arts Collective
LaToya Brooks, Founder
brooksartscollective@gmail.com
IG/FB @brooksartscollective

Block Band Music & Publishing,
LLC
D. Rashad Watters Founder,
CEO
(919)-698-2560
BlockBandMusic@gmail.com

AMMEA
President: Ernest Stackhouse
Email: ej.stackhouse@gmail.com
Website: www.ammea.org

TLW Photography
CEO/Founder: Taylor Whitehead
Email: mrknowitall91@aol.com

SC DJ WORM 803
CEO/Founder: Jamie Brunson
Email: scdjworm803@gmail.com
www.scdjworm803.com
@SCDJWORM803 - Twitter
@SCDJWORM803 - Instagram
SC DJ Worm 803 - Facebook
SC DJ Worm 803 – Mixcloud

The Black Techies/Podcast
CEO/Founder:
Herbert L. Seward III
Slogan: "Where black culture
meets the world of technology"
www.theblacktechies.com

themarchingpodcast.com

The Marching Podcast
CEO/Founder: Joseph Beard
Email Address:
marchingpodcast@gmail.com
Website:
www.themarchingpodcast.com

The Marching Force
www.supportthemarchingforce.com
Mailing address: The Marching
Force - 700 Emancipation Dr.,
Hampton, VA 23668.

Sugar Top Spirit & Beverage Co
CEO/Founder: Terri White
Email Address:
tl.white412@gmail.com
Website: www.sugartopspirts.com.
Twitter & Instagram
@sugartopspirits

PacketStealer Gaming
CEO/Founder: David
Matthews
Email Address:
packetstealer@outlook.com

The Urban Learning &
Leadership Center, Inc.

Urban Learning and Leadership
Center
President and Co-Founder
John W. Hodge, Ed.D
jhodge@ulleschools.com

MilRo Entertainment
Owner: Chevis Anderson
Email: milrosplace@yahoo.com

Assurance Tax & Accounting Group, LLC
CEO/Founder Kimberlee Collins-Walker
8676 Goodwood Blvd Ste 102
Baton Rouge, La 70806
Ph: 225-757-5518
Email: kim@assurancetaxbr.com
Website: www.assurancetaxbr.com

Southern University Alumni Federation
Address: 124 Roosevelt Steptoe Dr
Baton Rouge, LA 70807
Office Phone: (225) 771-4200
Email: sualumni@sualumni.org

Southern University A&M College
Address: 801 Harding Blvd,
Baton Rouge, LA 70807
Phone: (225) 771-4500

ACTIVate
Yladrea Drummond, J.D.
Email: contact@activateleadership.org
info@yladreadrummond.com
Website: www.yladreadrummond.com
www.activateleadership.org

J.Robins CPA, LLC
CEO/Founder Joseph Robins
9800 line Hwy Suite 261
Baton Rouge, LA 70816
(225) 650 - 7306
info@jrobinscpa.com
www.jrobinscpa.com
FB @jrobinscpa
IG @robinscpa

Courtney "Cici" Walker, MPA
Email: cicisfreelanceservices@gmail.com
Phone #: (225) 288-8216
Instagram: @cicisfreelanceservices

The Ancestor Key
CEO/Founder Ja'el Gordon
theancestorkey@gmail.com
504-356-1466

Derouen Services LLC
CEO/Founder Marina Zeno
Contact number: 337-418-0785 for business

Made in United States
North Haven, CT
05 April 2022

17928496R00161